TO:

FROM:

DATE:

Anne Neilson's CHRISTMAS ANGELS

Devotions & Art of Hope and Joy for the Advent Season

ANNE NEILSON

with poetry by Caroline Arey

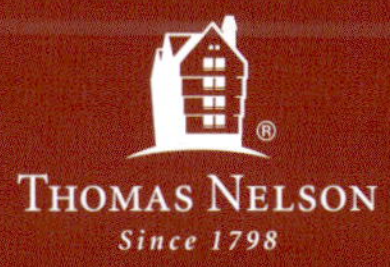

THOMAS NELSON
Since 1798

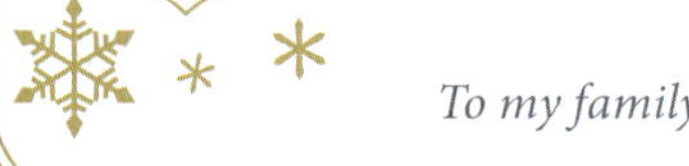

To my family—you are my everything!

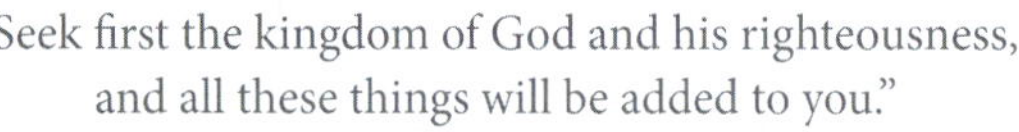

"Seek first the kingdom of God and his righteousness,
and all these things will be added to you."
MATTHEW 6:33 ESV

Pause, reflect, and redirect this Christmas season through scriptures, prayers, and art. As we enter a sacred season of preparation and expectancy, let us engage our senses to find renewed delight in our divine King.

Published in Nashville, Tennessee, by Thomas Nelson. Thomas Nelson is a registered trademark of HarperCollins Christian Publishing, Inc.

Thomas Nelson titles may be purchased in bulk for educational, business, fundraising, or sales promotional use. For information, please e-mail SpecialMarkets@ThomasNelson.com.

Cover design by Sabryna Lugge / interior design by Mallory Collins and Lori Lynch
All original art courtesy of Anne Neilson
Poetry by Caroline Arey, pages 2, 34, 66, and 98
ISBN 978-1-4002-3894-1 (hardcover)
ISBN 978-1-4002-3889-7 (audiobook)
ISBN 978-1-4002-3885-9 (ebook)

Printed in Malaysia

26 27 28 29 30 31 SEM 7 6 5 4 3 2

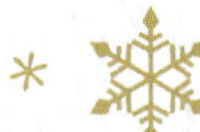

Contents

MARY'S SONG

My soul glorifies the Lord
and my spirit rejoices in God my Savior,
for he has been mindful
of the humble state of his servant.
From now on all generations will call me blessed,
for the Mighty One has done great things for
me—holy is his name.
His mercy extends to those who fear him,
from generation to generation.
He has performed mighty deeds with his arm;
he has scattered those who are proud in their
inmost thoughts.
He has brought down rulers from their thrones
but has lifted up the humble.
He has filled the hungry with good things
but has sent the rich away empty.
He has helped his servant Israel,
remembering to be merciful
to Abraham and his descendants forever,
just as he promised our ancestors.

Luke 1:46–55

Introduction

Our Response to the Ultimate Gift

When you think of Christmas, what comes to mind? For me there are many emotions: Anticipation. Joy. Peace.

And then there are the tears. My children will tell you that what they remember on most Christmas mornings is me crying. And I was not crying because my heart was tender toward a baby born to take away the sins of the world. No, I was crying because I was exhausted. Flat-out exhausted.

Most Christmas mornings, I had scurried around for weeks leading up to the magical day. Prepping the house to make it warm and inviting. Stringing thousands of lights on the Christmas tree only to have them fail to shine the moment I plugged them in. Shopping for the right gifts for each of my family members.

Early on, when my children were little, someone gave me the idea not to go crazy in the gift-giving department and to set expectations for only three gifts to each child—much like what the wise men brought the baby Jesus. What a great idea!

Yet that was really difficult for me to adhere to. When I went shopping, I kept purchasing little things, like a new set of pajamas or a cute pair of socks—whatever I thought my children might like. Those three gifts I intended to buy multiplied into a lot more, filling the space under the tree with so many presents.

On Christmas morning, always after reading the Christmas story in the New Testament, we would settle ourselves around the tree, and I would play Santa, distributing each of the gifts I had wrapped—those first gifts wrapped neatly and carefully, with folded edges taped just perfectly and adorned with tied ribbons and bows, followed by the hastily wrapped gifts with a simple peel-and-stick bow slapped on top.

EVEN THOUGH MY CHILDREN WERE JUST BEING CHILDREN . . . IN THOSE MOMENTS, I WOULD ENCOUNTER SOME OF THE HEAVINESS THAT CAN COME WITH THIS SEASON.

Then the complaining would start. I would hear echoes of "I didn't want this" and "Why did you buy this?" My heart would break, and after a few moments, the tears would start to flow. My children's complaints in the midst of an abundant, bountiful display of gifts would make me think of so many others going through Christmas without having much—like the people experiencing homelessness who were struggling on the streets, or people living paycheck to paycheck, or those with no gift to open at all. And even though my children were just being children (and great reminders of our humanity!), in those moments, I would encounter some of the heaviness that can come with this season.

My heart ached, not only for the people living on the street or those going without, but for my own family. I prayed that Jesus, the baby in the manger we were celebrating on this special day, would touch the hearts of my family. I prayed they would know that Jesus is enough, that Jesus is the *real* gift at Christmastime. I prayed He would save us from our pain, from our disappointments, from sickness and disease, from the hardness and the unfairness of life, and even from our own sometimes misguided hearts.

So you can see how I ended up in tears on so many Christmas mornings. But these times ultimately helped me recenter and refocus my family on Christ. Christmas gave each of us a chance to really embrace the gift of Jesus. So that is my prayer for you throughout this Advent journey.

Preparing Our Hearts for Jesus

I pray that you may be able to prepare your heart for this wonderful gift, that you may be able to open the gift of Jesus not just on Christmas Day but every day, and that you may be able to open your heart to the wonder of these gifts that came with a baby born in a humble barn.

Throughout this little Advent book, I am going to share stories, scriptures, and prayers as we prepare our hearts for Jesus. Each week has a focus—hope, love, joy, and peace—so that you can experience all that Jesus brings at Christmas, especially when you're feeling the lack of those four virtues. We'll look at the prophecies in the Old Testament—those moments of history that bring such wonder and revelation to my heart—that point to Jesus and that became flesh all those years later when the Christ child was born. We'll delight in the nativity story found in all four gospels and how those present at Jesus' birth offer a word for us today. And we'll pray that God increases hope, love, joy, and peace in our hearts as we reflect on the gift of Jesus.

IF YOU'RE SEEKING GOD THIS SEASON, YOU *WILL* FIND HIM.

If you're familiar with my art, you might know I love to paint angels. Painting these angels for this book gave me the opportunity to imagine what the nativity was like—what it would have felt like for Mary and Joseph, the shepherds, and the wise men to encounter angels at this most awe-inspiring time.

If you're seeking God this season, you *will* find Him. I believe that. And I pray that as you navigate this Advent journey, doors will be unlocked for you that will usher in peace in the midst of chaos, hope when your situation seems hopeless, love when you feel unloved. More than anything, I hope this season brings the joy and expectation that God goes before you and has a plan for you—and, as the prophet Jeremiah said, that plan is to bring you hope and a future (29:11).

With my art and my writing, I know I am called to be a light in this world, pointing people to Jesus and to the truth of God's Word. God is so big and can do some pretty incredible things, like having an angel visit a young virgin girl to tell her she would be carrying the Son of God. God can do amazing, miraculous things in your life too.

I pray that during this holiday season—through prayer, His living Word, and also through glimpses of my life and art—you will see a big God doing big things in your life. I pray that during this Advent season you will find the kind of hope, love, joy, and peace that only Jesus brings.

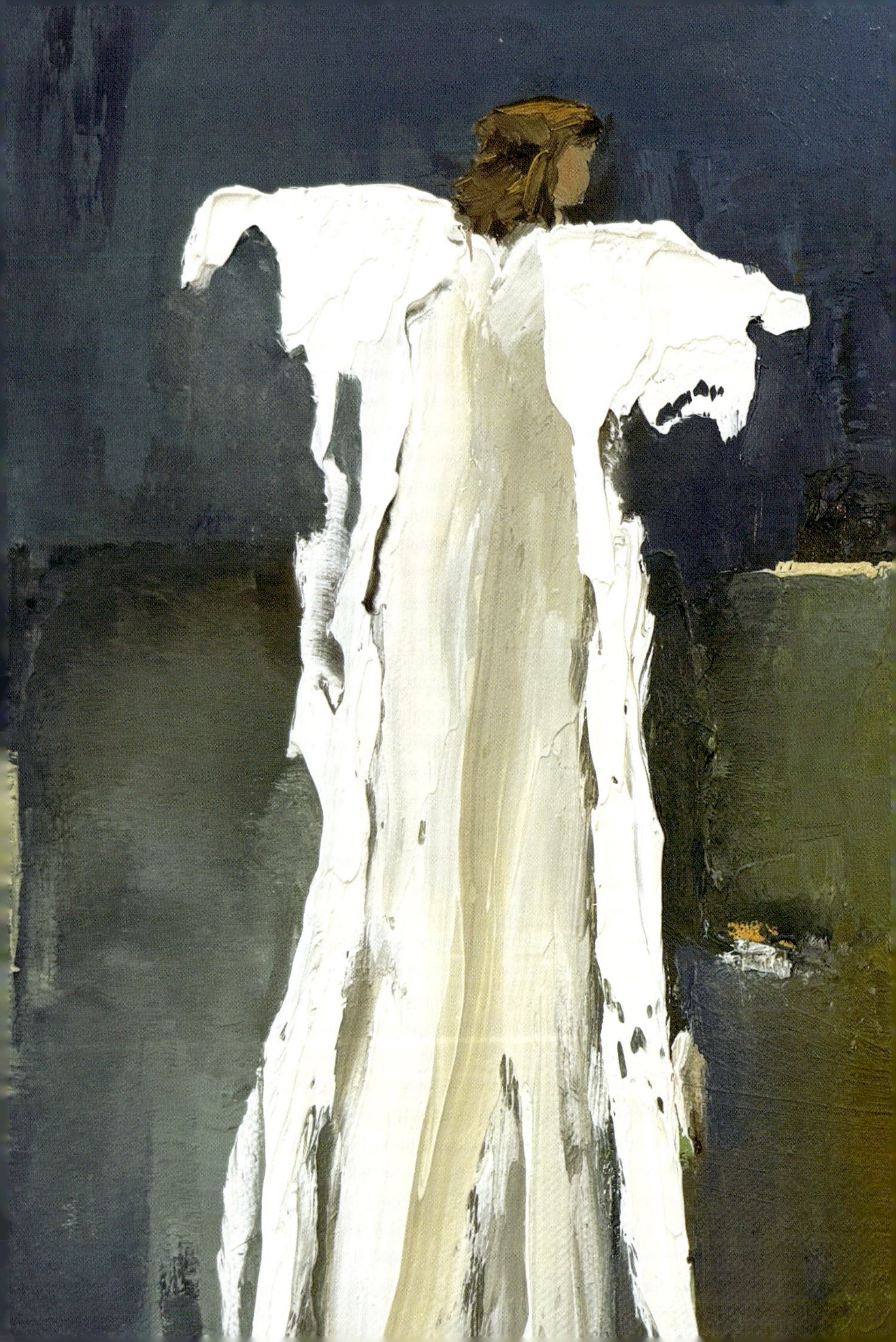

WEEK 1

Hope

The angels brought *hope* . . .

I look in her window and watch her pray on her knees,
A woman of the Lord seeking hope, faith, and peace.
I don't want to scare her as I slip inside,
But I have news to share, and God will be her guide.

"Mary, don't be afraid," I quietly but boldly say,
"A King you will birth in a manger of hay."
She looks confused, scared, but obedient in her call.
Oh, the glory that is to come that night in a horse's
stall.

I leave her then, but I keep watch in the days to come
As she and her husband, Joseph, prepare for
Bethlehem.
I cheer her on as she grows bigger and the day
draws near.
I silently embrace her as she and Joseph battle fear.

I'm close to them as they approach the keeper's place.
I know they're confused; I see the excitement fall from
Mary's face.
I prepare the barn that's meant for them,
And heavenly hosts seek the shepherds who will
worship Him.

The star shines bright above, sparkling because it knows
Tonight is the night that the earth will be saved from
its woes.
I hear a baby's cry break through the silent night,
And I call to my friends in heaven to join me in flight.

Above the flocks we gather with a message of triumph
and joy.
"Shepherds!" we announce with excitement. "Come see this
baby boy!"
And in that cold stall, suddenly rich with hope and peace,
Christmas has come in Him whose glory will never cease.

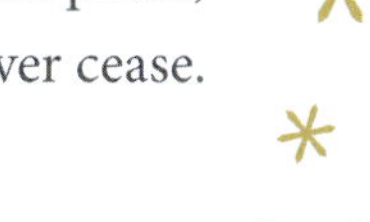

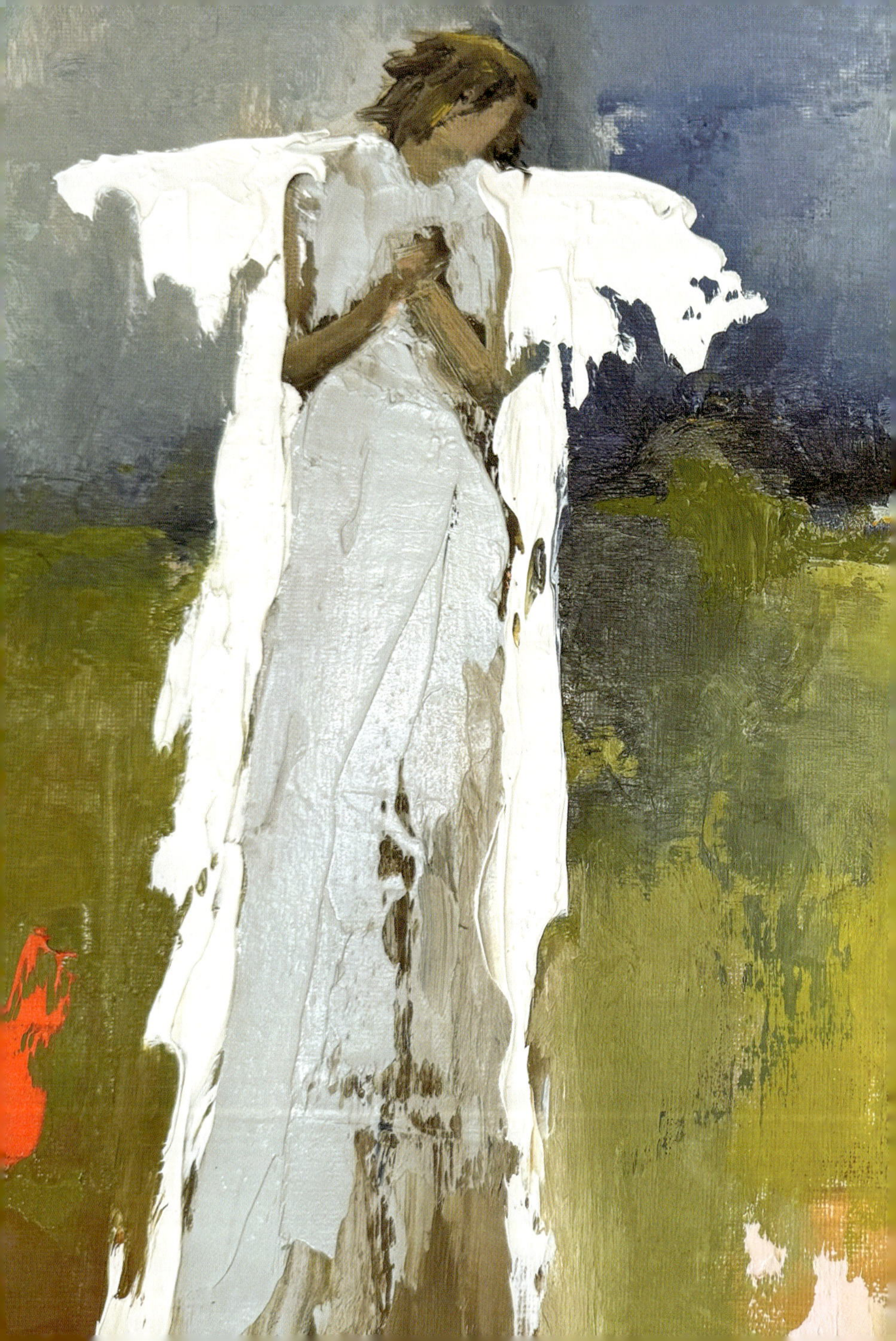

DAY 1

Hope in the Lord

Be strong and take heart, all you who hope in the LORD.

PSALM 31:24

What must have been going on in Mary's heart the night the angel came to deliver the message that she, an innocent young girl, would bring the Savior into the world?

My three girls are much older than Mary was at the time the angel brought this shocking news. I wonder what each of my daughters would have done or said if an angel had come to one of them and said she had been chosen to bear God's Son. What would have gone through her mind?

The obedience Mary displayed, plus her strength and hope in the Lord, are astonishing and admirable. Can you imagine this young girl going back to her family to tell them the news? She must have been terrified to face all the questions she knew would be coming . . . anxious about Joseph's reaction . . . fearful of judgment during that time in history. She would have needed great strength to face so many unknowns.

HE IS FAITHFUL TODAY AND ALWAYS.

We learn that Mary was "highly favored" by God (Luke 1:28). God saw her heart, a heart that hoped in the Lord, and He was faithful to her throughout her life.

God sees the hearts of His people too. He is faithful today and always. You might be going through a season where you need to be strong in the Lord, where you need to take heart and know that He goes before you and will be your hope in this world. Spend time today pondering what it means to take heart, to be one whose hope is in the Lord.

Early in this Advent season, let's pause and pray to the One who brings hope—right in the season *you're* in today.

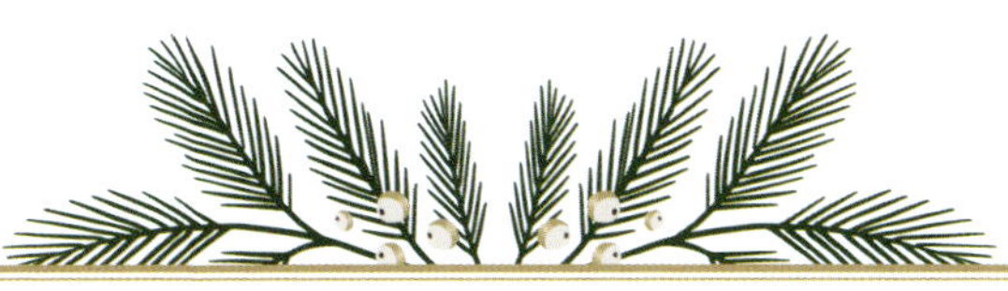

Dear Lord,

This is the first day of Advent . . . a time of waiting . . . a time of expectation. I pray that You would go before me this day and keep my eyes fixed on You and the mighty promises You have for my life. Where there is doubt, Lord, I pray that You would turn it into trust. Where there is pain, Lord, wrap Your arms around me and carry me through. You and You alone are my strength, and I will find rest in You. Today, Lord, my hope is in You. Thank You for walking alongside me, and thank You for Your promises.

In the name of Jesus,

Amen.

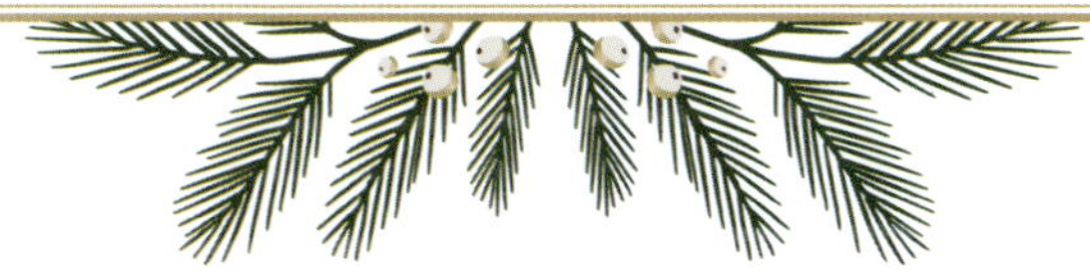

DAY 2

Be Not Afraid

Lift up your voice with a shout, lift it up, do not be afraid; say to the towns of Judah, "Here is your God!"

ISAIAH 40:9

I don't know about you, but the global COVID-19 pandemic and the years since have been so strange for me. The fear, the sadness, the misinformation at times, the unknown—it's all been overwhelming and jarring.

My mom, who is a mighty prayer warrior, always talks about "the woes of the world," increasingly so in the past few years. I do believe we are living in some surreal times that aren't in line with biblical truth, but what I always tell my mom is that God is on the throne with Jesus at His side. They aren't up in heaven, pacing back and forth, wondering what to do next. They are seated and victorious, watching what we do on this earth.

Are we wearing out the soles of our shoes as we anxiously worry about what's happening in the world? Or are we trusting in the Lord and putting our hope in Him? Are we acting based on what we hear in the news, or are we turning to God's Word and trusting Him for all things? Are we heeding the command that appears so many times: "Fear not"?

THE SON HE DELIVERED TO US WILL CALM YOUR FEARS, QUIET YOUR MIND, AND BRING YOU HOPE.

Today, I pray that you would set aside anything that worries you, anything that fills your heart with anxiety. I pray that you would surrender those things to the Lord, who is seated on His throne and waiting for you to turn to Him. The Son He delivered to us will calm your fears, quiet your mind, and bring you hope.

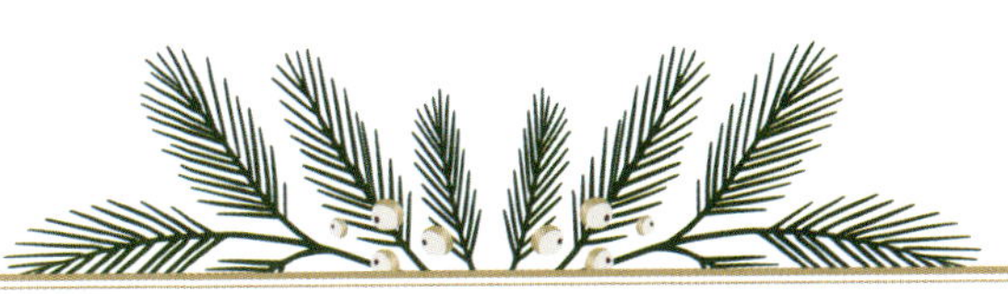

Dear Lord,

I surrender my heart to You today. Anything and everything that might be weighing me down, Lord, I surrender to You. I choose to trust in You and Your Word. I choose to cling to hope even though everywhere I look seems hopeless. Bring peace in the midst of the storm. I give You glory for what You've done and for what You will continue to do. You are my strength and my hope. I will cling to that today, no matter what.

In the name of Jesus,

Amen.

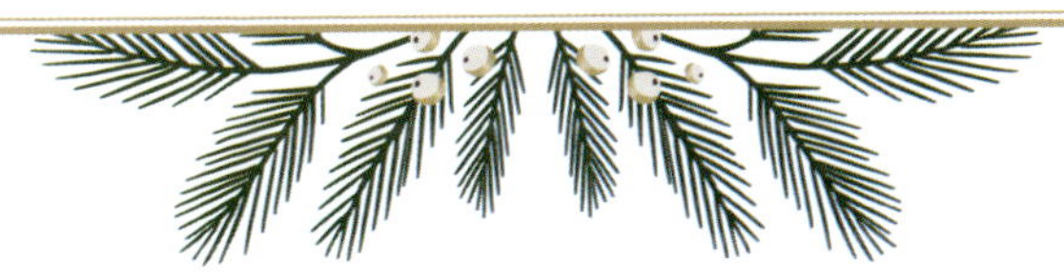

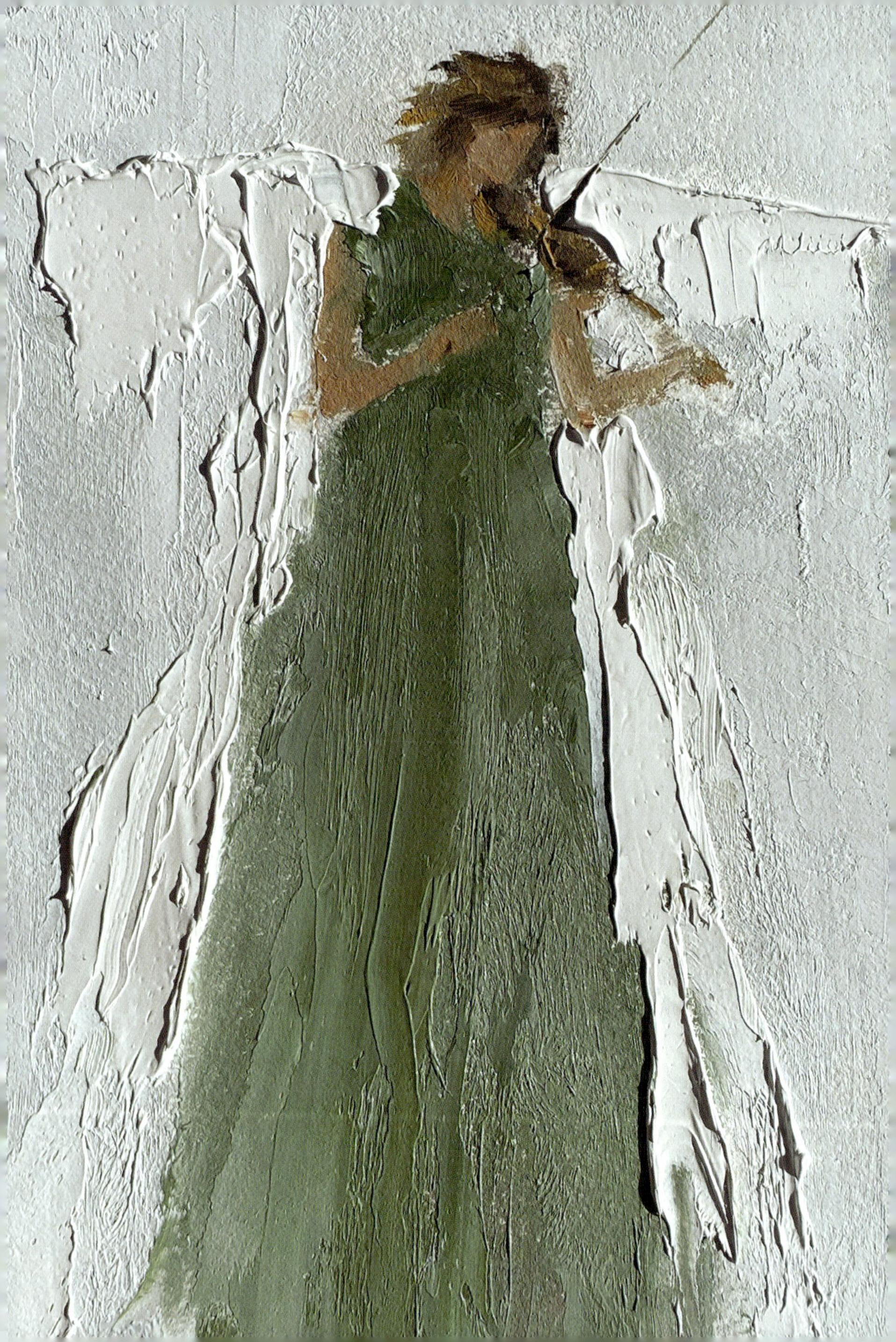

DAY 3

Overflowing

May the God of hope fill you with all joy and peace as you trust in him, so that you may overflow with hope by the power of the Holy Spirit.

ROMANS 15:13

Even though I grew up in the church, I didn't know much about the Holy Spirit. My mom was "baptized in the Holy Spirit" when I was a teenager and consequently dragged my sister and me to some healing services where people spoke in tongues. As a teenager I was mortified by this seemingly strange behavior and had no idea what was going on. But as an adult, when I had a personal encounter with the Holy Spirit, my perspective on Him changed completely. I was awed by the power of the Holy Spirit, His presence, His ability to touch me in real and powerful ways.

The Holy Spirit's role in the Trinity, not only during the Advent season but every day, is so integral to our lives as believers. The Trinity is, admittedly, a difficult concept to grasp, but I used to explain it to my children when they were younger in this way: Visualize God as if He were the three components of water—liquid, ice, and steam. The Trinity is similar; it is three different parts but the same thing: God the Father, God the Son, and God the Holy Spirit. What an incredible gift to humankind—that we have access to the Father, the Son, and the Holy Spirit all the time!

HE WILL BE YOUR HOPE THIS SEASON.

Years ago, I had a surreal moment while visiting Turkey, when I stood in the very same church where the Nicene Creed was written and where it had been agreed upon that the Trinity consisted of God the Father, God the Son, and God the Holy Spirit. Chills ran down my spine as I stood inside those ancient walls. I could feel the Spirit's power then, just as I can now.

Spend time today opening your hands and your heart and surrendering to the Holy Spirit. I pray that He will pour forth into your life and empower you in all that you do and that He will be your hope this season.

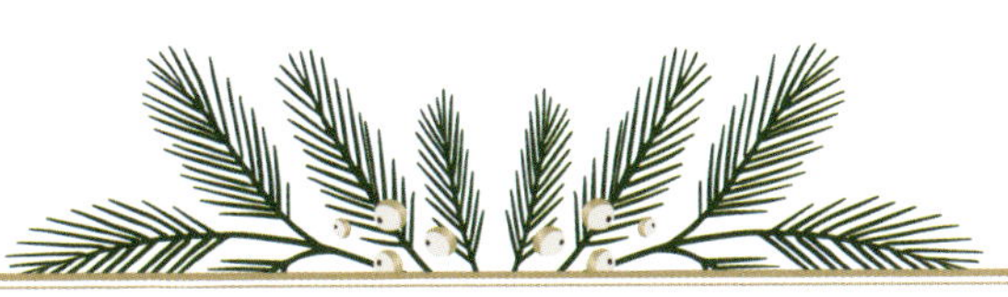

Lord,

I open my hands today to receive the Holy Spirit as a gift to me from You. I empty every part of my being in order to be filled with the power and the hope of the Holy Spirit, from the tips of my toes to the top of my head. Lord, fill me up. Fill me until I am overflowing. Cleanse my heart of any doubt. Cleanse my heart of anything that would hinder the work of the Holy Spirit in my life. In faith I receive the gift of the Holy Spirit and trust that You will empower me on this faith journey.

In the name of Jesus,

Amen.

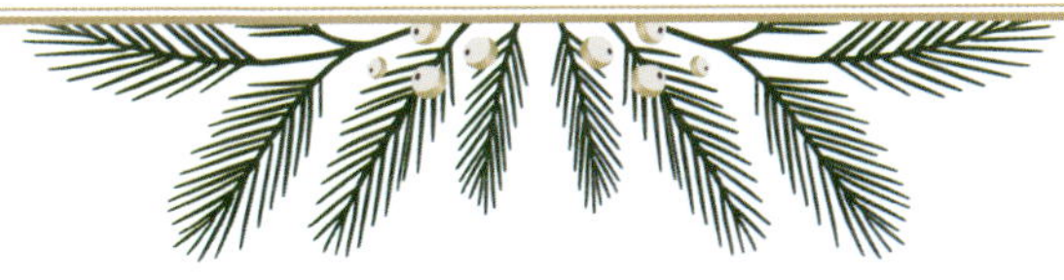

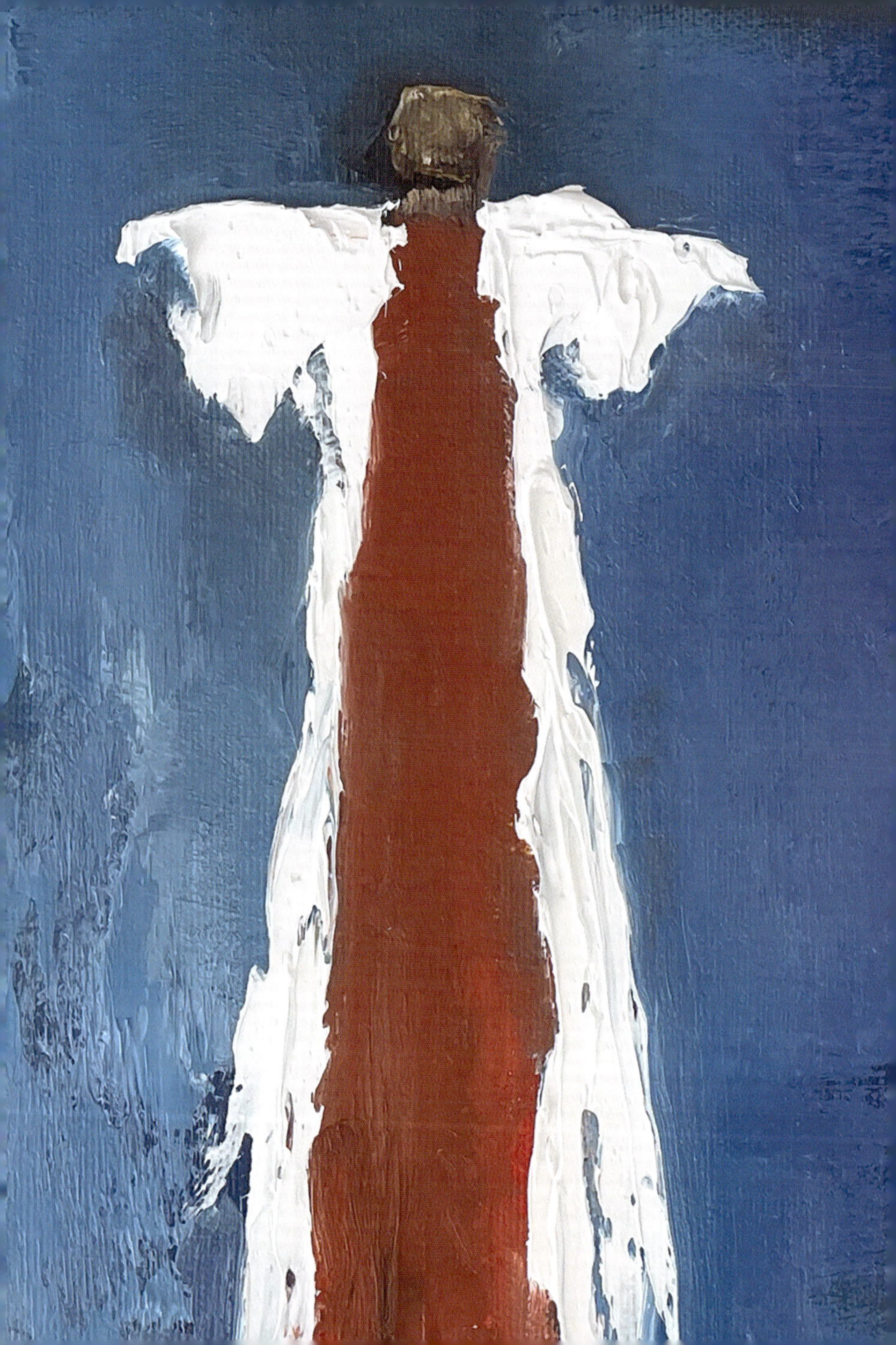

DAY 4

Refuge in His Word

You are my refuge and my shield; I have put my hope in your word.

PSALM 119:114

I will never forget when my mom became a born-again believer. I was fifteen years old, and she would tell me to open my Bible to any random page and just read what God wanted to say to me. Just open the Bible, point, and read.

This may not be your approach to reading the Bible, but looking back on that practice, I can see how God does speak through His Word in even the simplest of ways—and especially for those new to opening a Bible in the first place. God's Word is not confined by a reading plan! It is living and active and sharper than any double-edged sword (Hebrews 4:12).

On the days when I need most to seek the Lord's refuge, there is no better starting point than opening up my Bible. I go to His Word on a daily basis, document what is going on in my life, mark the highs and lows and everything in between as I drink of God's truth. I pray that all of my many Bibles, scattered all over my house, will be a legacy for my children. I hope someday they will open the pages and see my handwritten prayers and pleas to God—how I needed Him to be my refuge and my shield for my marriage, my children, our circumstances, anything that I was going through. I hope they see how I clung to His Word.

HE IS YOUR SHIELD AND REFUGE—TODAY AND ALWAYS.

Many of my notes are in the Psalms, a source of great hope for me. My practice is to read a psalm, allow God's Word to sink deep within my soul, and then journal my pains, my hopes, and my dreams.

This Advent, whatever season you might be going through—loss, despair, wonder, joy—my prayer is that you would open up His Word and find hope. Make notes in the margins of your Bible so you can go back later and see the hand of God moving in your life. He is your shield and refuge—today and always.

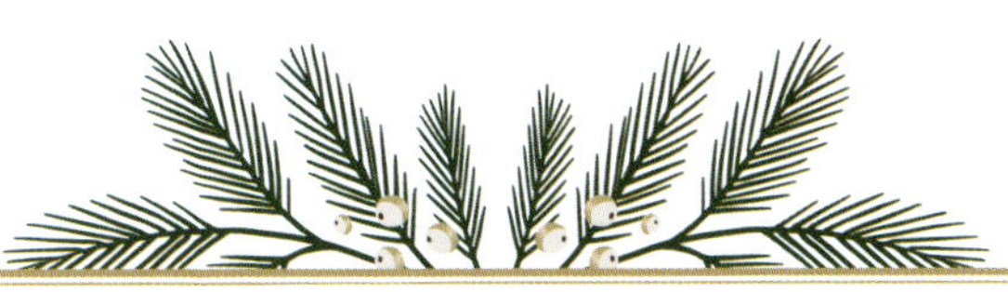

Dear Lord,

Your Word is living and active and sharper than any double-edged sword. I come to You today with an expectant heart, believing that You will speak to me through Your Word. I pray that You would comfort me, that You would guide me, that You would show me the way in which I should go. Speak to me through Your living Word. And when I don't understand, I pray that the power of the Holy Spirit would reveal Your truth in my life. Today, as I go about my day, I pray that You would give me a word to cling to—a promise that You have for me. Let me find refuge in You and Your unfailing love.

In the name of Jesus,

Amen.

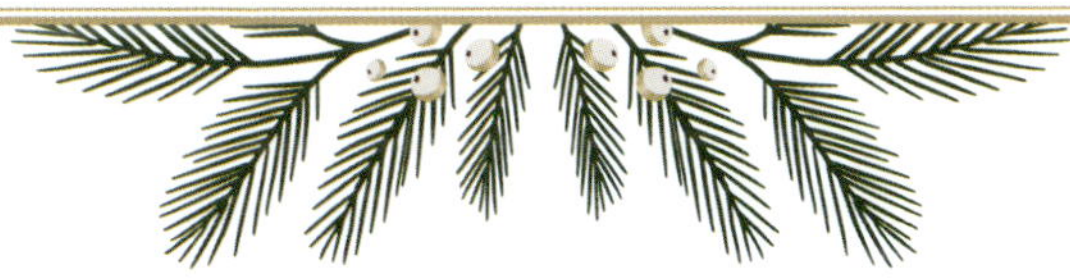

DAY 5

Faithful to His Promises

Let us hold unswervingly to the hope we profess, for he who promised is faithful.

HEBREWS 10:23

Take a moment and ask yourself the following:

Where is my hope today?
Is it in the world, or is it in the living Lord Jesus?

Putting our hope either in the world or in our circumstances is sure to leave us disappointed—not to mention discouraged. But if we put our hope in the Lord? He will *never* disappoint. He who promised is faithful.

We may inherently know this truth, but it can be so difficult to remember! We see purpose, meaning, fulfillment, and legacy in so many earthly endeavors—including our jobs, our marriages, our children, our achievements, our government, our communities, our circumstances. But when those things let us down, which they inevitably will, what do we do? Where do we turn? In whom do we trust?

HIS PROMISES TO YOU ARE FAITHFUL NO MATTER WHAT YOUR CIRCUMSTANCES ARE TODAY.

This Christmas season I pray that you will redirect your hope. If your hope is in something other than Jesus, I pray that you will let that something go, that you will instead turn your eyes toward the manger and the baby who was born to take away the sins of the world. Jesus will take your hand if you will grab hold of His. His promises to you are faithful no matter what your circumstances are today. His promises to you are *yes* and *amen*. Grab ahold of the hope in Jesus. He is faithful.

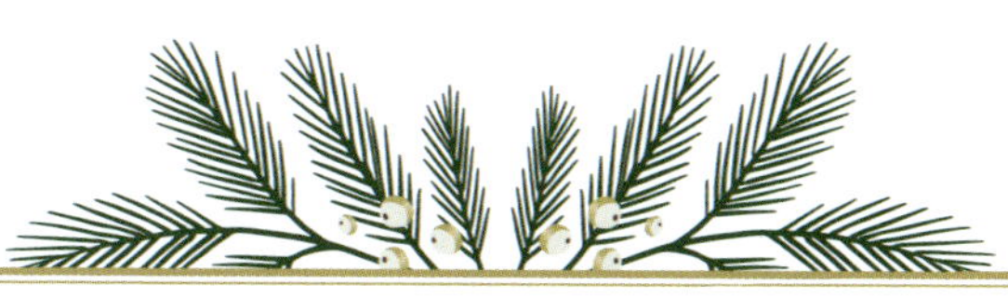

Dear Lord,

I want to redirect my focus today. I want my focus to be on You and only You. I pray that You would set my eyes on Jesus, the author and perfecter of my faith. I pray that my hope, today and every day, would be solely in You. I pray that I would not look to the past or compare myself to others, but instead look to You and trust that You will carry me through this day no matter what comes my way. If I am clinging to something that is not of You, Lord, let me know when and how to let it go. I want to cling only to You in my life. I thank You that You are my everlasting hope.

In the name of Jesus,

Amen.

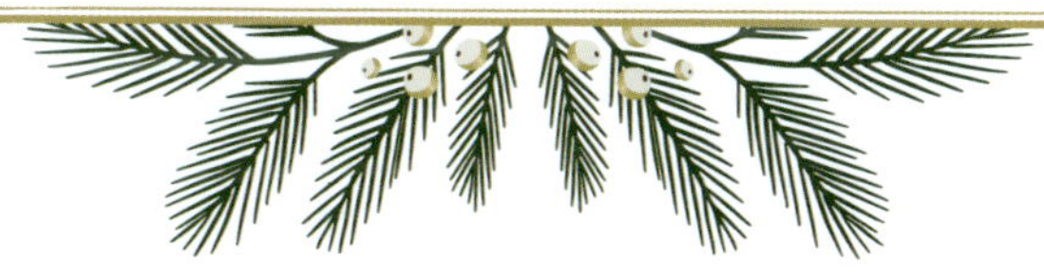

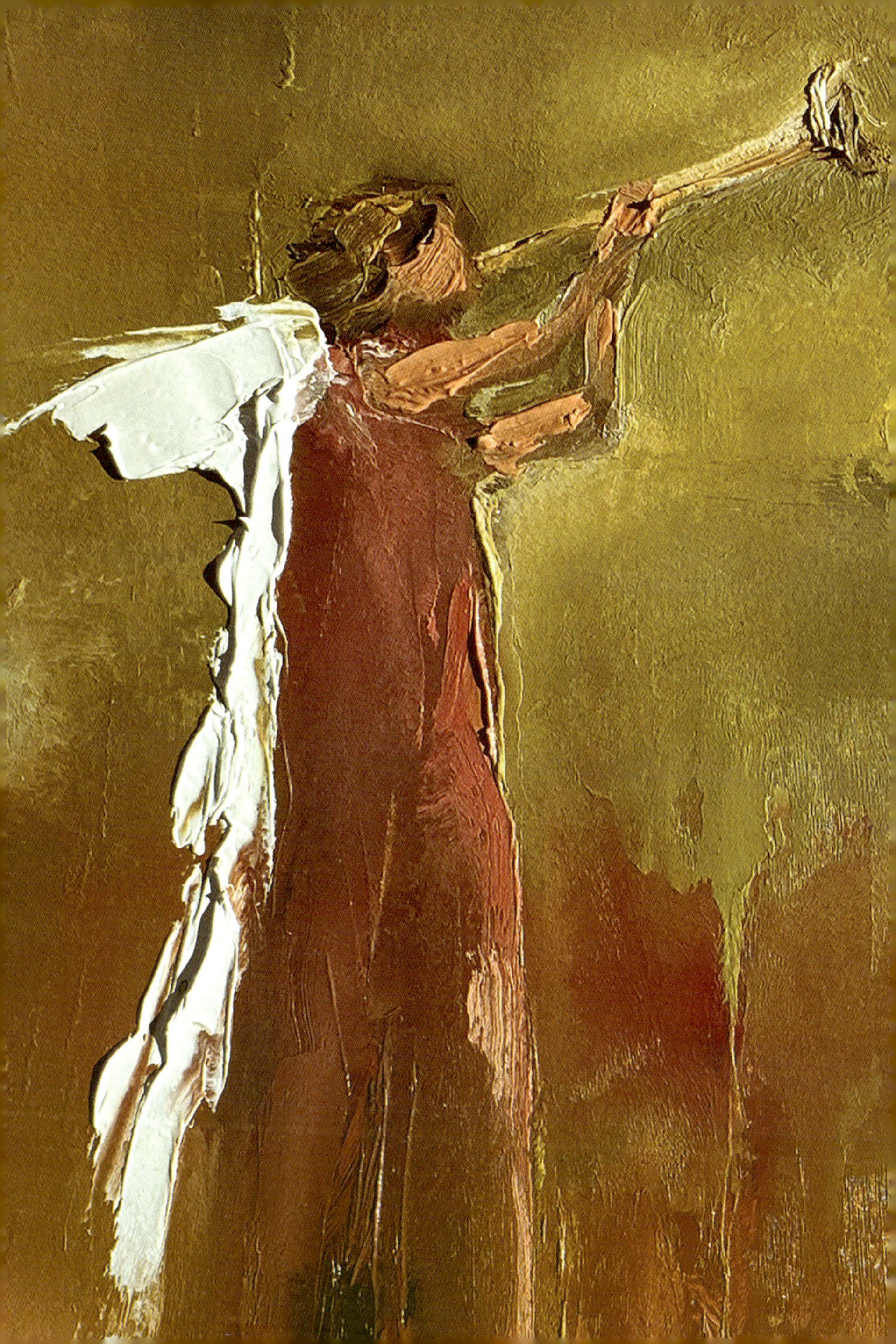

DAY 6

Waiting on the Lord

I wait for the Lord, my whole being waits, and in his word I put my hope.

Psalm 130:5

Waiting. Oh, that word—*waiting.*

Waiting can feel so endless sometimes. So hard. So painful. Waiting on a doctor's report, waiting on a wayward child to return, waiting those nine months to deliver a baby. Even waiting at the DMV can feel never-ending! And yet in the difficulty of waiting, God wants us to press into His presence, to wait patiently and expectantly before His throne, to come to Him with thanksgiving—even as we wait on His promises.

Think of Mary, Jesus' mother. As she grappled with the shock of being told that she would carry and give birth to the Son of God—the Lord of lords, the Messiah who would take away the sins of the world—she entered her own season of waiting. As she grappled with this news, she put her hope in the Lord's promises as the days and months passed, while a baby was growing in her belly.

Advent is a season of great rejoicing, but sometimes our circumstances don't allow us to feel very joyful. Whether you're in the midst of a difficult season or your own time of waiting, God's promise doesn't change. He is present, He is near, and He is in the waiting.

YOU CAN REST AND REJOICE AS YOU PLACE YOUR HOPE IN THE LORD.

What promise are you waiting on from God? Spend today rejoicing that He is faithful and His promises to you are true. You can rest—and rejoice—as you place your hope in the Lord, who goes before you in all things.

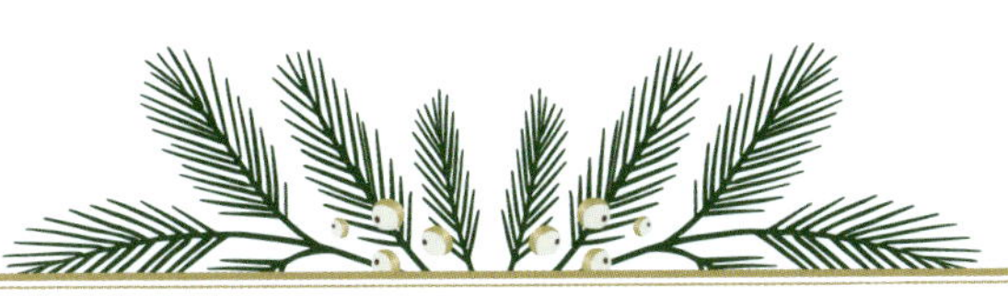

Precious Lord,

I lift up to You everything I am waiting for. I know that Your timing is perfect, today and always. Teach me to sit in Your presence and not try to rush things along. Help me to trust in the Holy Spirit and not the "hurry-up spirit." I know that our world wants everything done fast, but let me trust solely in You and Your timing. As You marinate the things in my life, I know they will turn out sweeter and more tender. I am grateful that I can surrender and trust in Your perfect timing for all my needs. I praise You for all that You are doing in my life. Even if I cannot see how or why or when, I will continue to trust.

In the name of Jesus,

Amen.

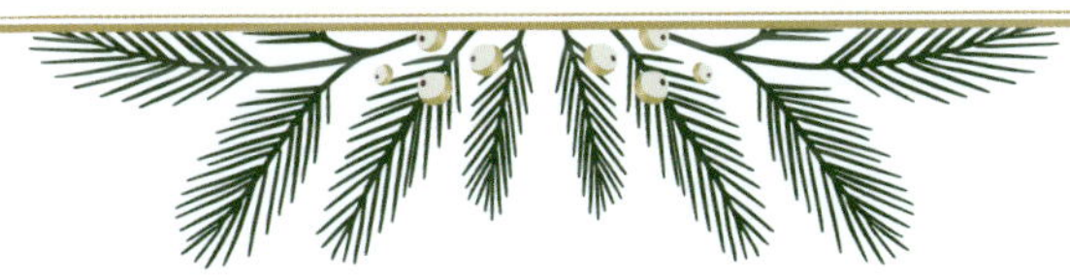

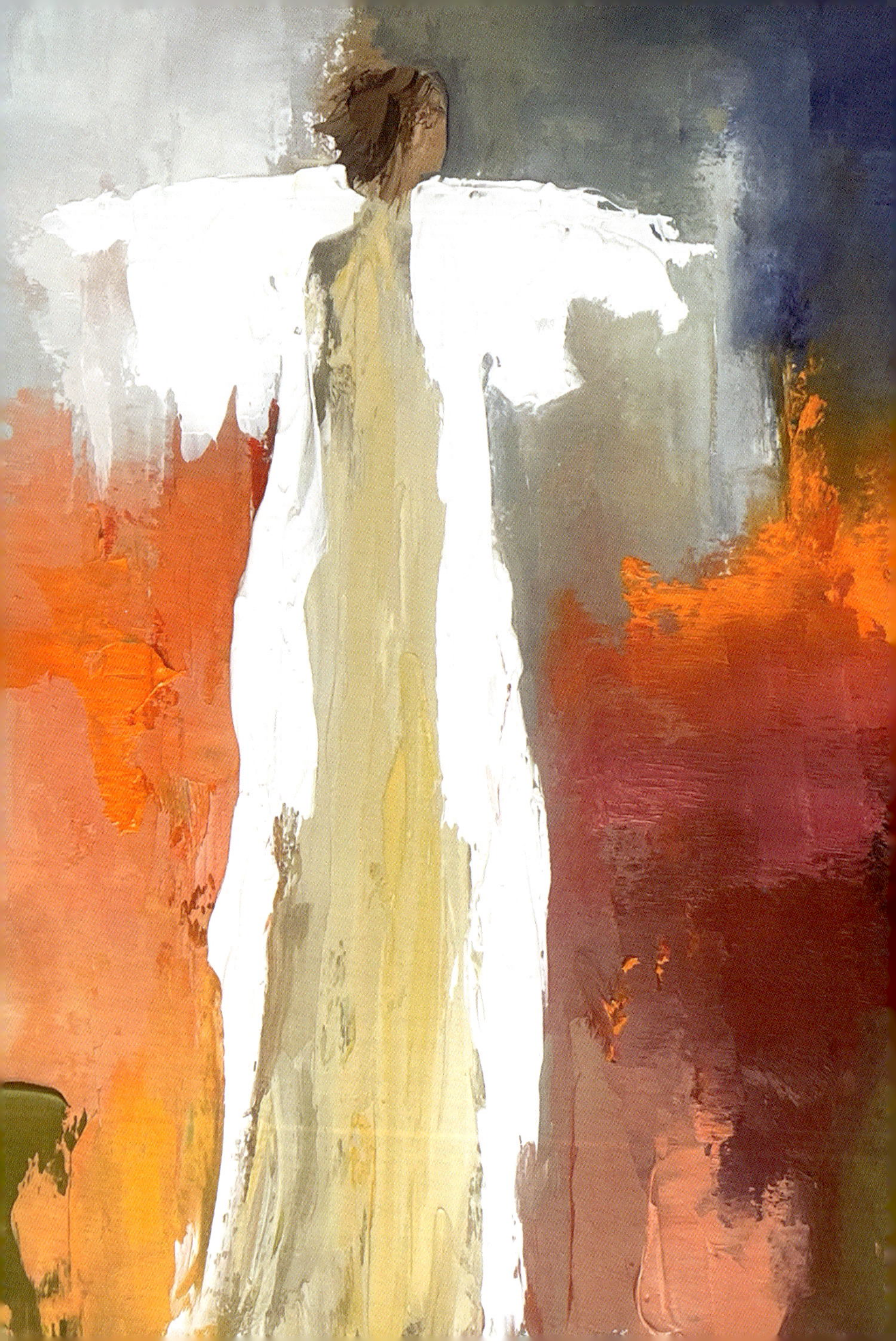

DAY 7

Perfect Faithfulness

Lord, you are my God; I will exalt
you and praise your name,
for in perfect faithfulness you have done
wonderful things, things planned long ago.

Isaiah 25:1

This week of Advent, we have been focusing on hope—what hope means to us, how we can cling to hope despite our circumstances, how we can have hope in the living God and in His Word, and how we can hope while we wait.

All of this hoping is possible because God is faithful to keep His promises. We see this all throughout the Bible.

On that very first Christmas, God sent His only Son, Jesus. In this miraculous act, God kept His promises from the Old

Testament prophecies. From Micah 5:2 we know Jesus was born into the tribe of Judah in the region of Ephrathah in the town of Bethlehem: "But you, Bethlehem Ephrathah, though you are small among the clans of Judah, out of you will come for me one who will be ruler over Israel, whose origins are from of old, from ancient times." And from Isaiah 7:14 we know that He was born from a virgin: "Therefore the Lord himself will give you a sign: The virgin will conceive and give birth to a son, and will call him Immanuel."

REJOICE THAT HE IS SOVEREIGN. HIS WORD WILL NEVER RETURN VOID.

God kept His promises then, and He will be faithful in keeping His promises to you now. Today, rejoice and give Him thanks for your circumstances. Rejoice in His perfect plan. Rejoice that He is sovereign. His Word will never return void. Even though you might not see it all clearly right now, hold on to hope and know that He is faithful and always keeps His promises.

Oh, rejoice in Jesus—the hope of the world!

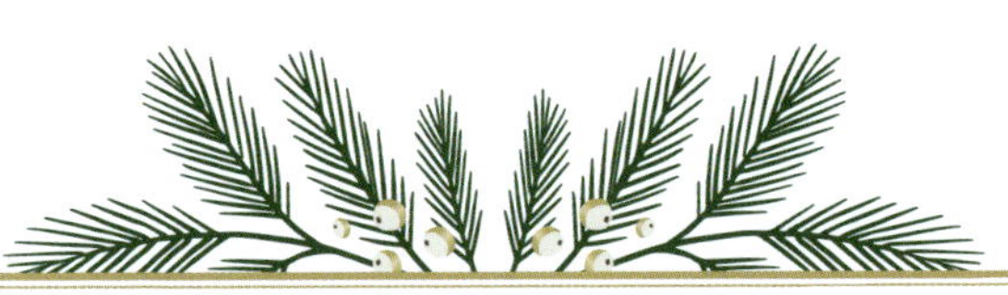

Dear Lord,

As I surrender my day to You, I cling to Your hope and Your promises for my life and all the things that I am praying for. No matter what, I have the assurance in Your living Word that You are sovereign and Your Word will not return void. I cling to that promise, and I thank You for Your perfect faithfulness. I thank You for the hope that I have in You and You alone.

In the name of Jesus,

Amen.

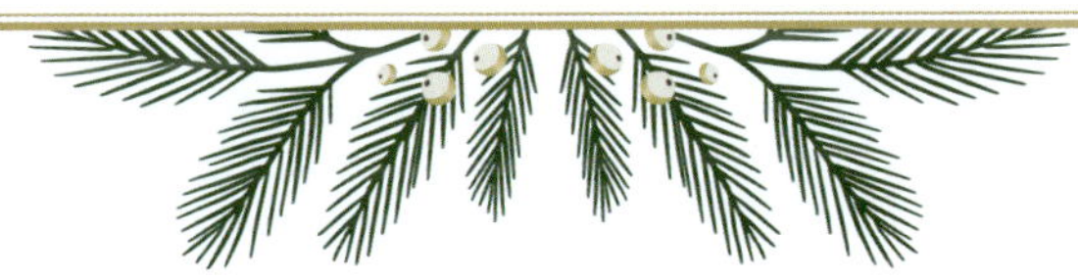

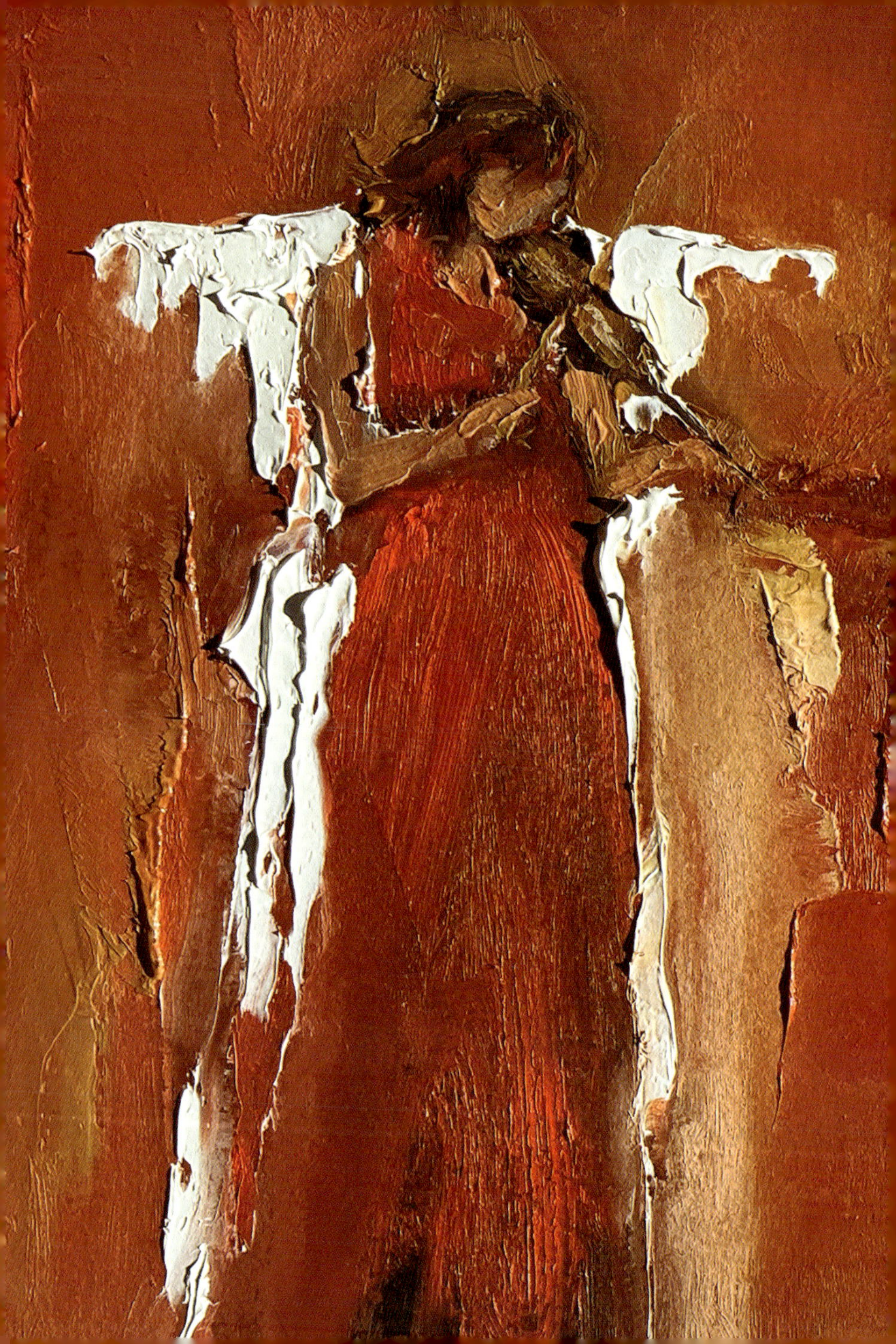

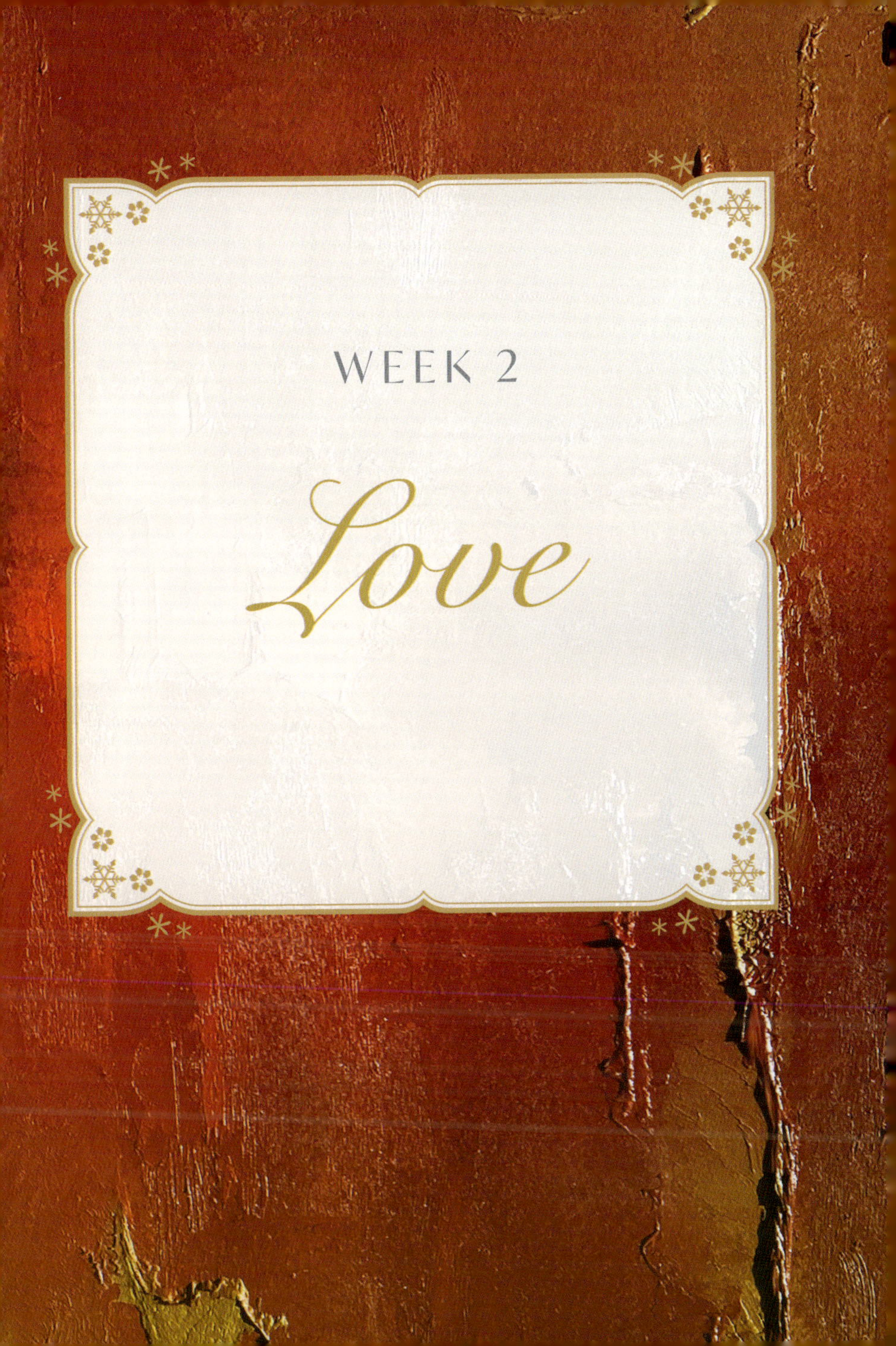
WEEK 2
Love

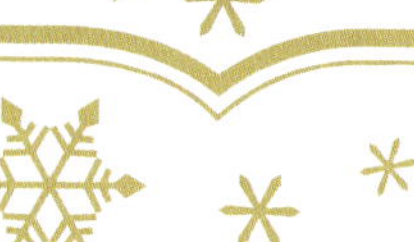

The angels shared the *love* of God . . .

It's glittering and bright, a haven full of worship and praise,
God on the throne, Jesus at His right hand, peace upon
God's face.
"It's time," the Father says, confident and sure.
"You must redeem the world—only You are perfect
and pure."

And so the Prince leaves heaven, the realm of endless grace,
To become a human infant, embodied in a less majestic place.
His early days are mysterious, closer to heaven than we
could ever know.
His arrival gives a bridge to Glory—from the Kingdom to
us below.

A humble carpenter to be His father; an obedient virgin to
be His mother,
Choices so simple and ordinary, but a grand plan for all
sinners to recover.
Christ's divine Father, determined to rescue us with love,
Gave a gift of His only Son—noble, perfect, sent from above.

And so He came in the most painful yet ordinary way,
A barnyard filled with animals, dirt, straw, and strands of hay.
Like any baby, He cried as breath rushed into His lungs,
And that breath changed eternity, rivers of righteousness
forever sprung.

His tiny body swaddled in cloth, humble and not quite clean,
An ordinary choice for the would-be Savior and King.
Nestled gently into Mary, a tiny weight upon His mother's chest,
A baby carrying salvation, resurrection, the promise of
perfect rest.

Like any mother, Mary poured herself out for her precious gift.
Did she realize her love was preparing the stage for the ultimate
cosmic shift?
His death would be remarkable, would trade a manger for a tree,
A Christmas gift that leads to Easter—from child to eternity.

Oh, the wonders of His love!
"He rules the world with truth and grace
And makes the nations prove
The glories of His righteousness
And wonders of His love,
And wonders of His love,
And wonders, wonders of His love!"[1]

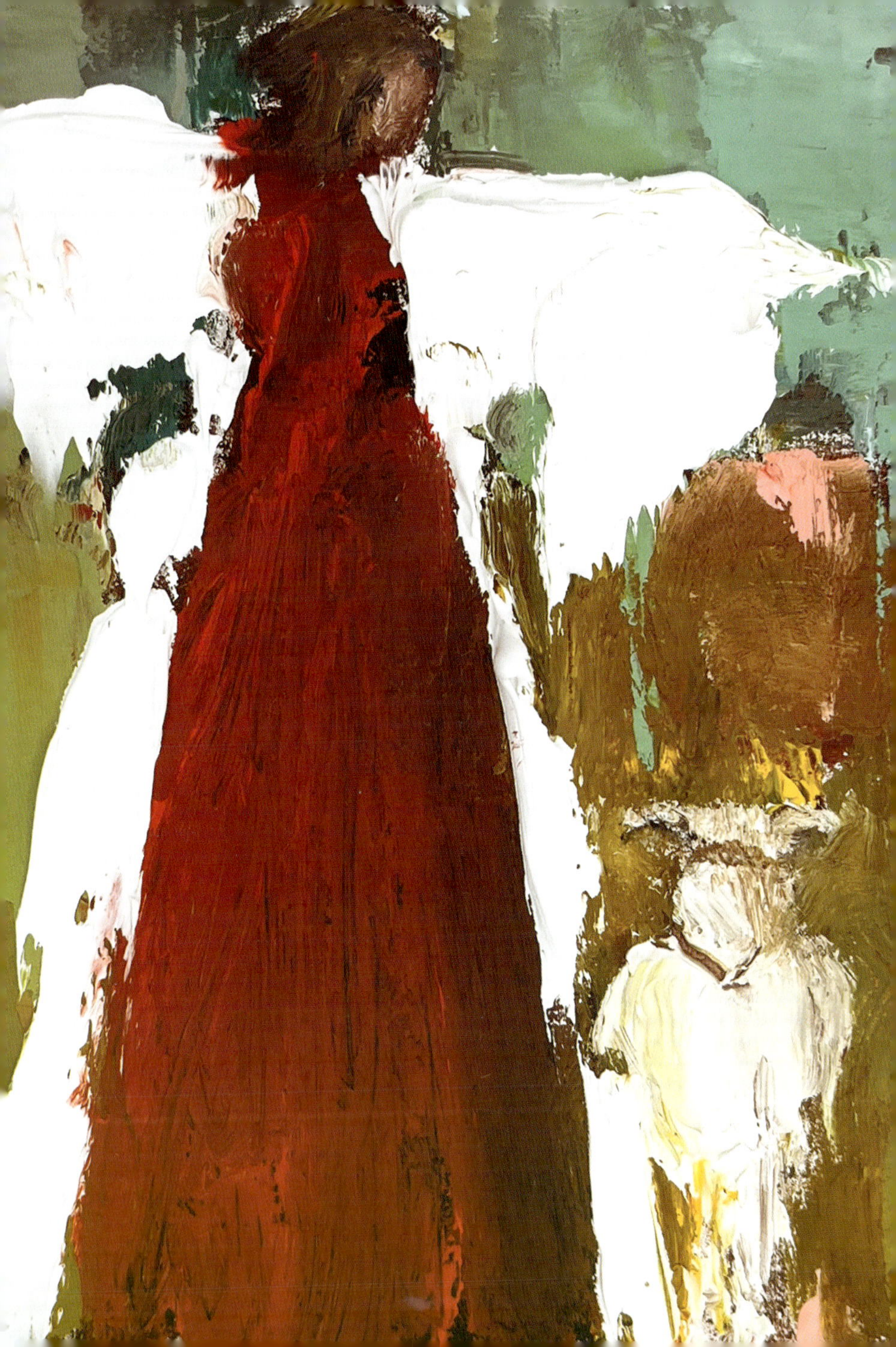

DAY 8

He Loves You More

This is love: not that we loved God, but that he loved us and sent his Son as an atoning sacrifice for our sins.

1 JOHN 4:10

For years, almost every morning I would write an encouraging note to my husband and my children, and I would sign it "I love you . . . but God loves you even more." I wanted them to know just how much He loves them every day, whether they are feeling grumpy or happy, whether they are late or on time, and whether they are put together or falling apart.

Pause for a moment and let this sink deep into your soul: *God loves you no matter what.* Do you believe that?

That truth might be difficult to accept for some of us who

feel like we don't deserve God's unconditional love. But today's verse makes it plain: It is not that we loved Him first. He loved us first—and still loves us now and will always be wooing our hearts closer to His.

I pray that today you will know that nothing is required of you to receive the love of the Father—including good deeds or cleaning yourself up or trying to be a better person. You cannot earn His love. Not by attending church every Sunday or serving more. None of that will make God love you any more than He already does.

> HE WILL WAIT PATIENTLY UNTIL YOU KNOW THAT HE LOVES YOU—UNCONDITIONALLY.

His only desire is for you to surrender to Him and trust Him for all things in your life. God wants your whole heart, and He will wait patiently until you know that He loves you—unconditionally.

Spend some time today resting in the arms of Jesus. Speak to Him as if He is holding you tightly. Give Him your heart, and let the power and presence of the Holy Spirit fill you up today!

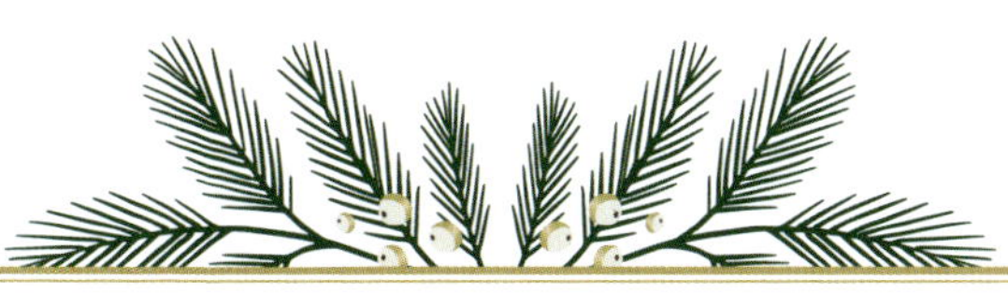

O precious Father,

It is completely humbling that You love me, flaws and all. You love me despite my wandering heart. You love me when I try to walk away. You love me when I try to hide my face from You. In those moments, You love me even more. I am ever so grateful today for the magnitude of Your love. I thank You that You continue to draw my heart to Yours, that nothing can separate me from the love You have for me. I know that nothing I do will earn or lose Your love, so let me just rest in Your loving arms.

In the name of Jesus,

Amen.

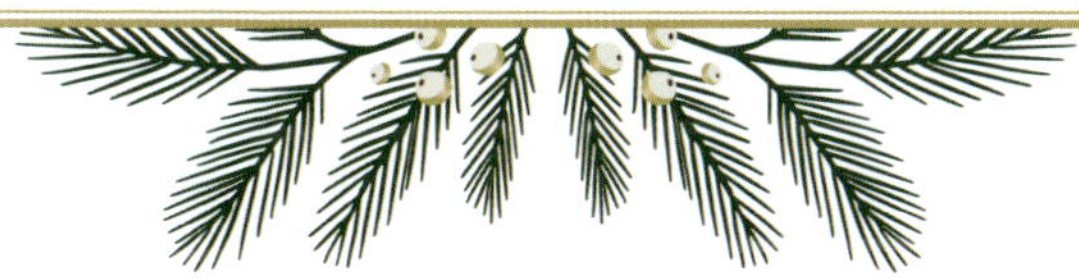

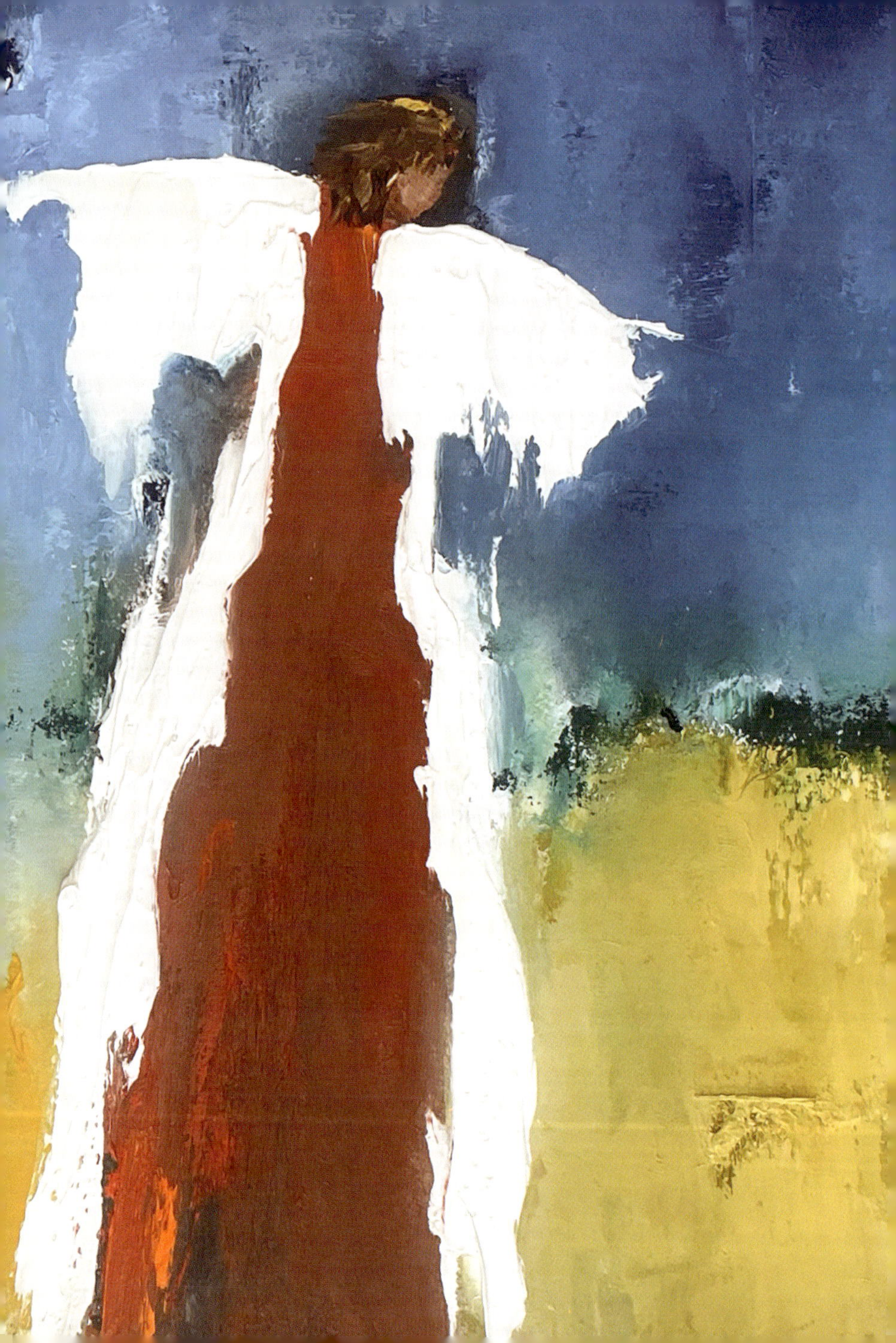

DAY 9

Compassion That Never Fails

Because of the LORD's great love we are not consumed, for his compassions never fail.

LAMENTATIONS 3:22

What does compassion look like to you? Years ago, I published a coffee-table book called *Strokes of Compassion*. The stories inside were full of compassionate encounters, some in the most unlikely places.

One of my favorite stories involved a cranky waiter and a handful of my close friends I was out for dinner with. We could tell early on that the waiter clearly didn't want to deal with our table of four loud, talkative women. His annoyed manner, his hurried check-ins, everything short of an outright eye roll—we knew he had no interest in giving us much time or attention.

Then one of my dearest friends leaned over to me and said, "Watch this. We are going to change this man's heart." And with each subsequent visit he made to fill glasses or bring our meals, my friend made every effort to get to know him. She was persistent in learning his name, where he was from, how long he had worked at the restaurant, all sorts of personal questions. And with each offering of compassion to that busy, overworked man, we saw his heart change. By the time we left, my friend had made a new friend and had brightened that waiter's day.

LET HIS LIGHT SHINE THROUGH YOU TODAY!

That is how God is with us—persistent and full of compassion. He tenderly and tirelessly works to extend compassion and change our hearts.

Take time today to find ways to demonstrate love and compassion to those who need it most. Even if you're out rushing around to get last-minute shopping done or running errands, this is a great opportunity to show compassion. Let His light shine through you today!

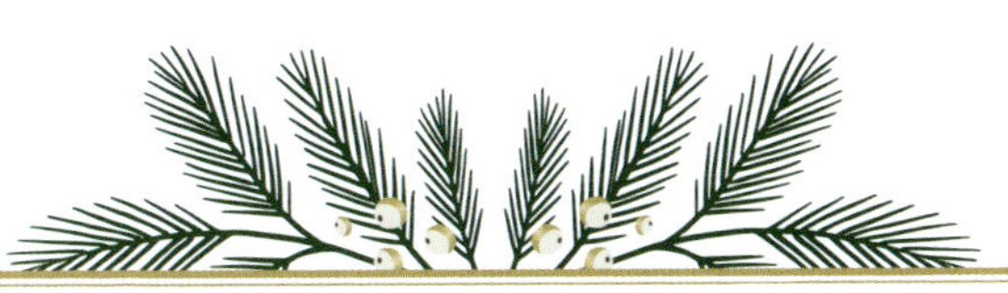

Precious Lord,

I pray for opportunities today to show compassion to others. I want them to see the light of Jesus shining through me. I pray that today I will be clothed with compassion, kindness, humility, gentleness, and patience in all that I do. Thank You for equipping me to be the hands and feet of Christ.

In the name of Jesus,

Amen.

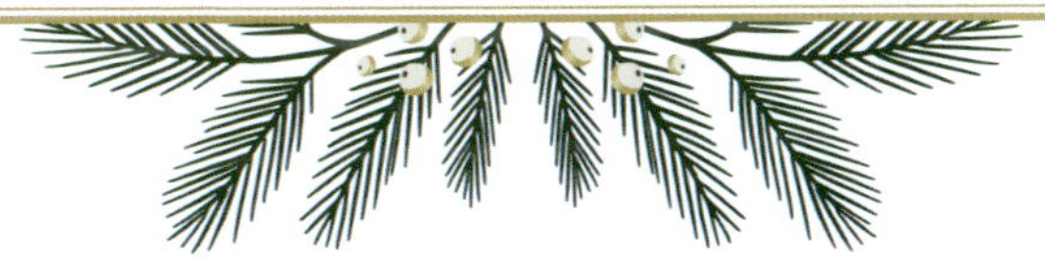

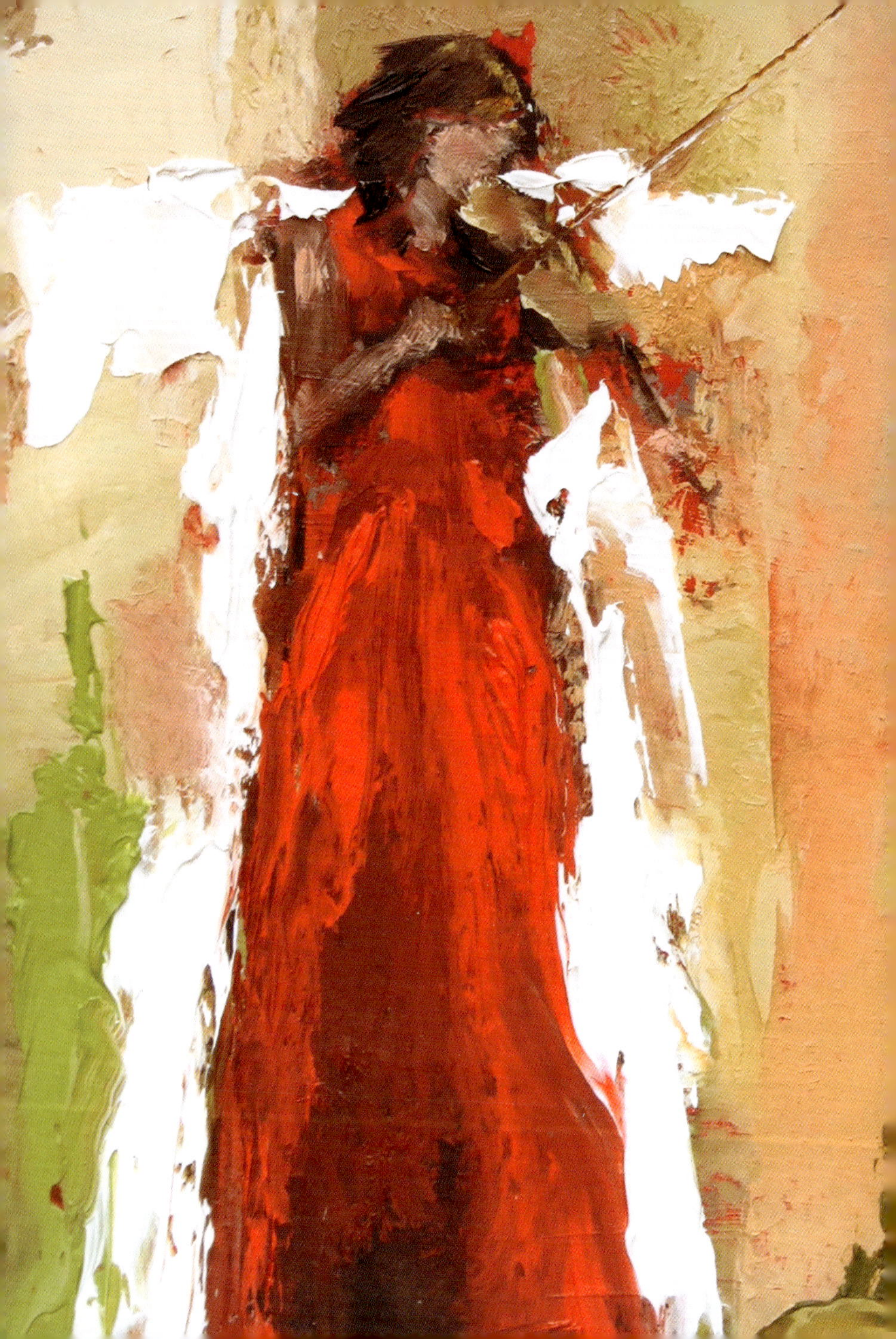

DAY 10

Sacrificial Love

Jesus looked at him and loved him. "One thing you lack," he said. "Go, sell everything you have and give to the poor, and you will have treasure in heaven. Then come, follow me."

MARK 10:21

Our English word *love* comes from the Greek word *agapao*, which means "to be fond of."[2] But the word is not just about fondness; it also carries the implication of selfless, sacrificial love.

When I think of sacrificial love, I think about the love God has for the world—not just for me in the United States of America at this moment in time but for the entire world, for all people in all places across all times. God's love all those years ago was so sacrificial that when He sent Jesus to earth to be born in a manger, He already knew His Son would ultimately have to die and the type of horrendous death he would endure. And yet God did not hesitate to show this kind of love for the world.

I cling to so much in this world—my image, my marriage, my children, my art—and sometimes I wonder if I would be willing to sacrifice it all for Him. Am I willing to surrender everything to Him and trust Him no matter what?

HIS WAYS ARE SO MUCH BETTER THAN OURS.

As you navigate through this season of Advent, anticipating the coming Lord, spend some time in prayer and ponder the things in your life you cling to that God might be asking you to offer to Him. What can you hand over to God today? I can promise you, if you do surrender it in faith, He is trustworthy to receive it. His ways are so much better than ours. Every time I let go of something I've been clinging to, His peace covers me in a powerful way. God might not be asking you to sell everything you possess, but He is asking you to open your hands and heart and turn everything over to Him.

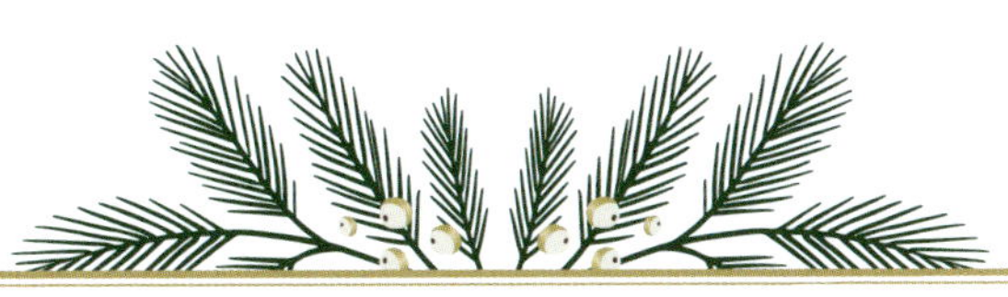

Dear precious Lord,

It can be so difficult to let go of my worries and cling to You, to truly surrender and trust in You. I pray today that the power of the Holy Spirit would move on my heart and show me the areas where I need to let go so I can cling to You instead. Reveal anything I need to hand over to You. I come with open hands and an open heart. Especially today, during this season of expectation, I surrender all to You. I cling to Your promises and trust in You.

In the name of Jesus,

Amen.

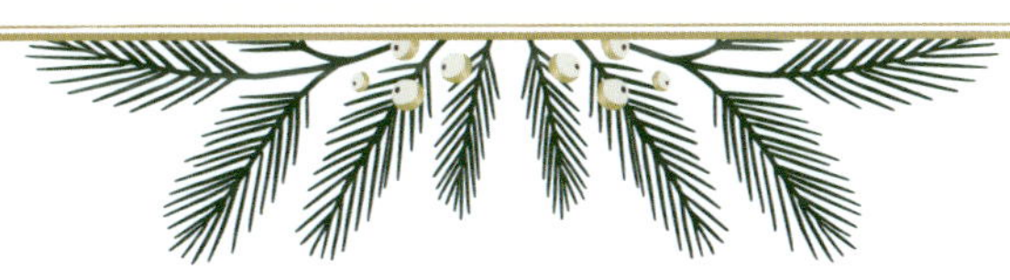

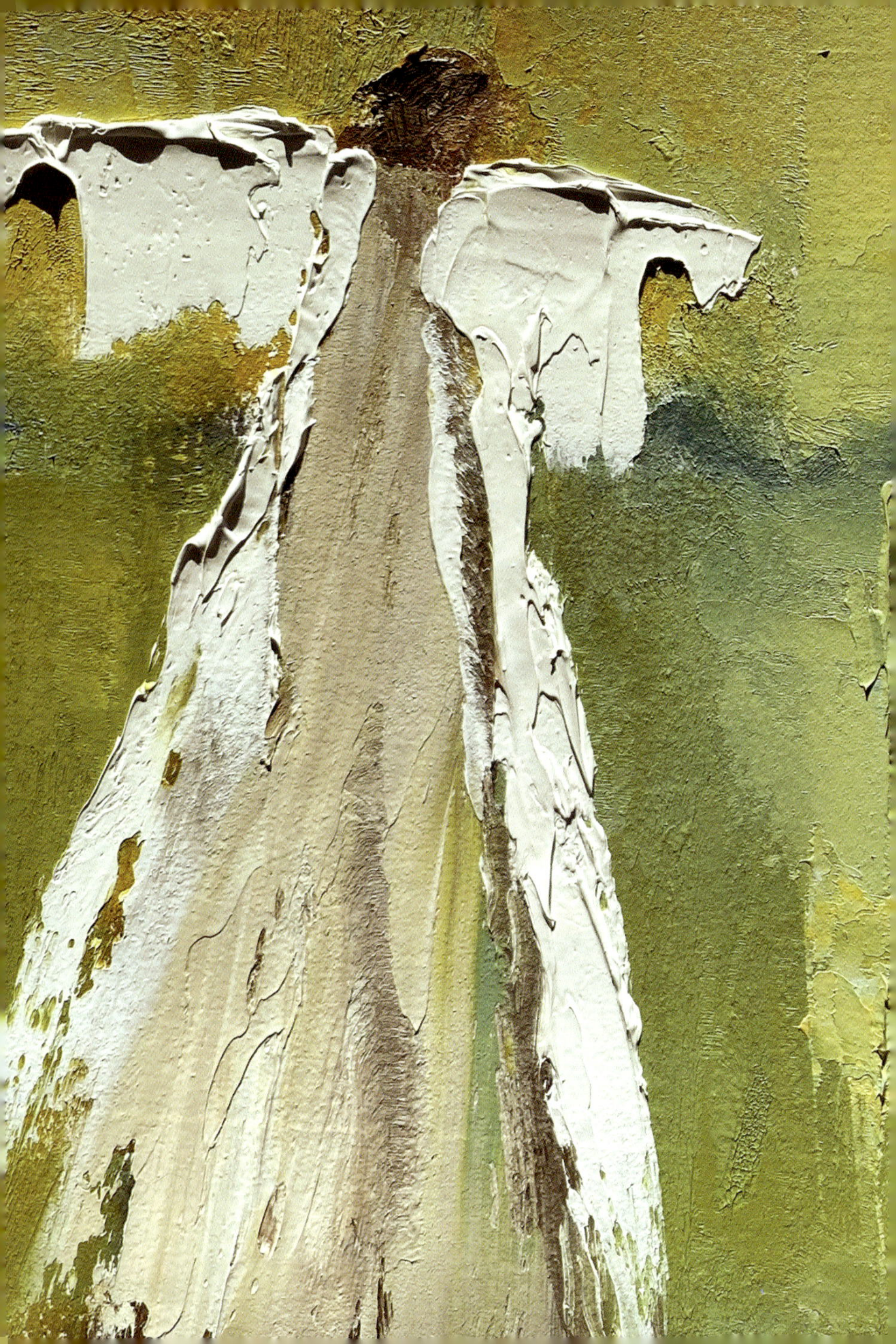

DAY 11

The Gift of Eternal Life

For God so loved the world that he gave his one and only Son, that whoever believes in him shall not perish but have eternal life.

JOHN 3:16

We often think of Easter as the season when we most experience the sacrifice of God's great love for us. After all, that's when Jesus died on the cross for you and me.

But Advent is also a time to consider the sacrifice of God's great love for us. During Advent we prepare our hearts not only for the birth of Jesus but also for the birth that leads to His death on the cross. How can we even begin to wrap our minds and hearts around the full scope of what Christmas means?

When new parents have their first child, they make many

special preparations: creating a registry, planning a shower, setting up a nursery, picking out the coming-home outfit. So many details and considerations, both big and small, go into welcoming a baby home.

LET US CONSIDER THE SACRIFICE, THE VICTORY, AND THE GREATEST LOVE THE WORLD HAS EVER KNOWN.

When I imagine those tender moments in heaven as God was preparing for Jesus to come to earth as a vulnerable newborn, I also think of how He was preparing for His only Son to experience pain and suffering and sacrifice—all for the sake of love.

May we bring a little of Easter into our Advent experience this year. Let us consider the sacrifice, the victory, and, above all, the greatest love the world has ever known. As you prepare gifts for your family, to show them your love this holiday, meditate on the careful, detailed time the Father spent preparing the world's greatest gift.

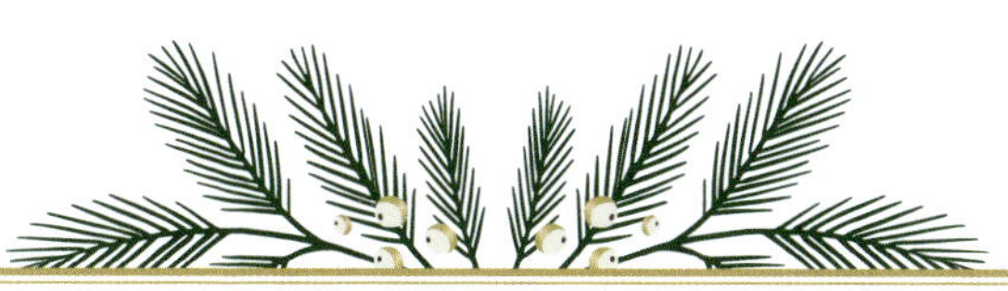

Dear precious Lord,

I ask that You prepare my heart today for Your Son. "Create in me a pure heart . . . and renew a steadfast spirit within me" (Psalm 51:10). I want Jesus to rule over all areas of my life. I am so grateful that this was Your plan from the beginning—to give Your only Son to sacrifice His life for me. I can hardly wrap my head around that kind of love, and I ask that You continue to draw my heart to Yours. Open my eyes to the wonder of Your love.

In the name of Jesus,

Amen.

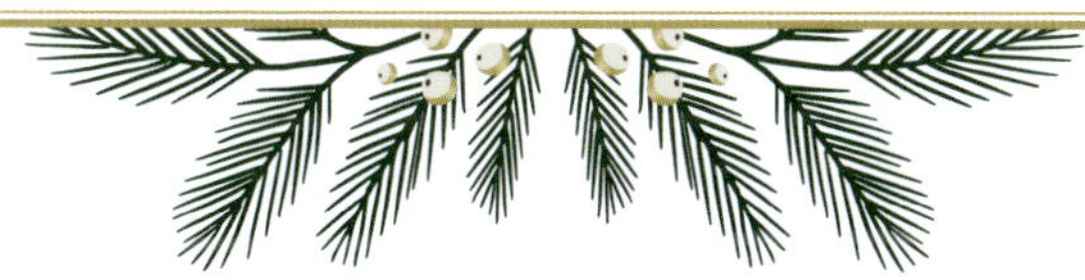

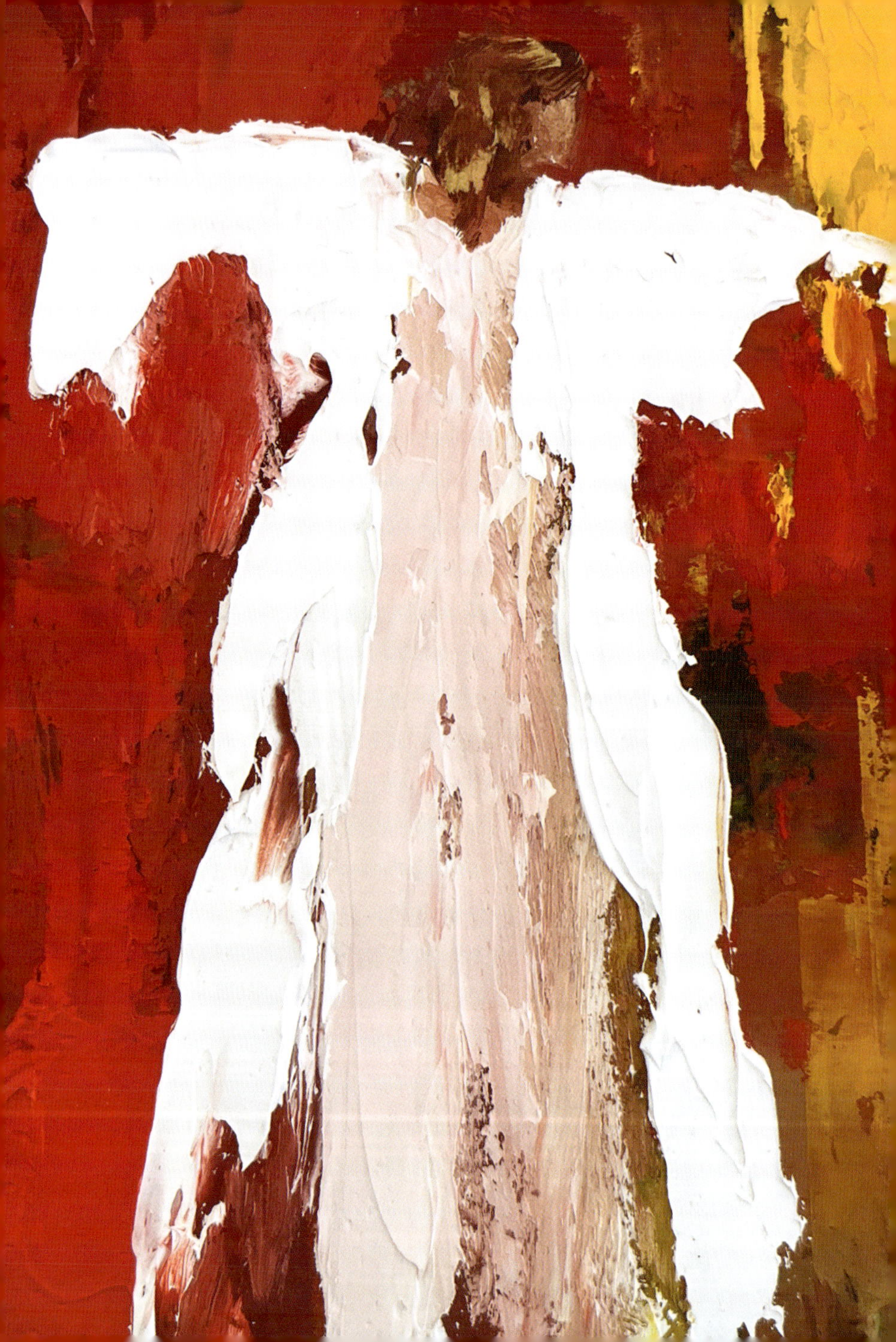

DAY 12

His Grand Love

See what great love the Father has lavished on us, that we should be called children of God! And that is what we are!

1 JOHN 3:1

Christmas morning is such a fascinating time of before and after. All the beautifully wrapped packages and the picture-perfect living room landscape you spent countless hours and weeks preparing . . . in mere moments they are ripped to shreds. Debris is scattered across a floor that was spotless just moments before.

And next year we'll do it all again. We'll shop and craft and bake and decorate. And after the careful preparations are turned into chaos once again, we'll do it all again the next year . . . and the next.

Imagine, if you will, God carefully planning for His creation, making scenes of joy and hope and peace, all wrapped in beautiful packaging. And then we sinners take only moments to destroy what He curated.

HIS LOVE IS GREATER THAN ANY MESS.

And yet, without hesitation, He does it all again. He sweeps away the rubble and mess and wipes the slate clean—ready to usher in more opportunities for hope and joy and peace. And above all else, He does it for more opportunities to showcase His grand love for us—over and over again.

This Christmas morning, as you survey the mayhem, remember that God is surveying your life, and He's ready and waiting to reset it again tomorrow.

His love is greater than any mess.

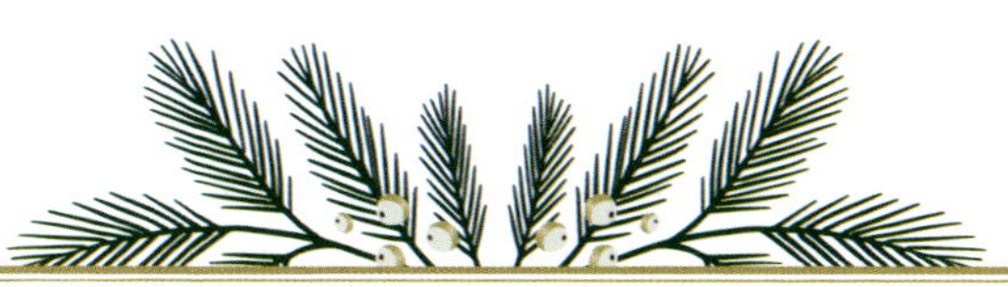

Dear Lord,

I come before You today and ask that You would quiet my heart in the chaos of life. I want to hear Your still, small voice whisper to my heart that I am loved by You—and that I needn't worry about anything else today. I pray that You would fill me up with Your perfect love so I can go about my day pouring out Your love to all those I encounter. I want Your light to shine through me in all that I do. Thank You for Your perfect love.

In the name of Jesus,

Amen.

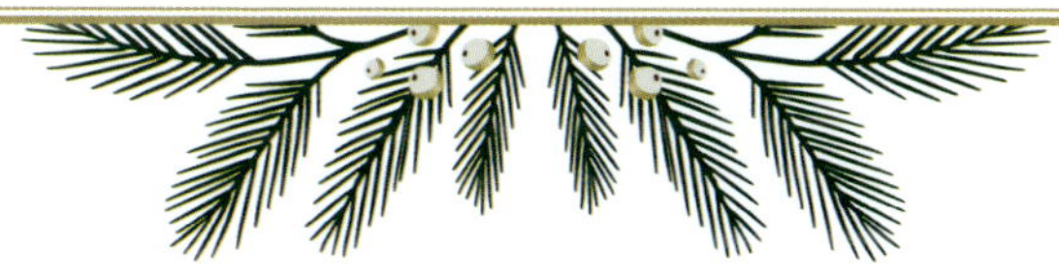

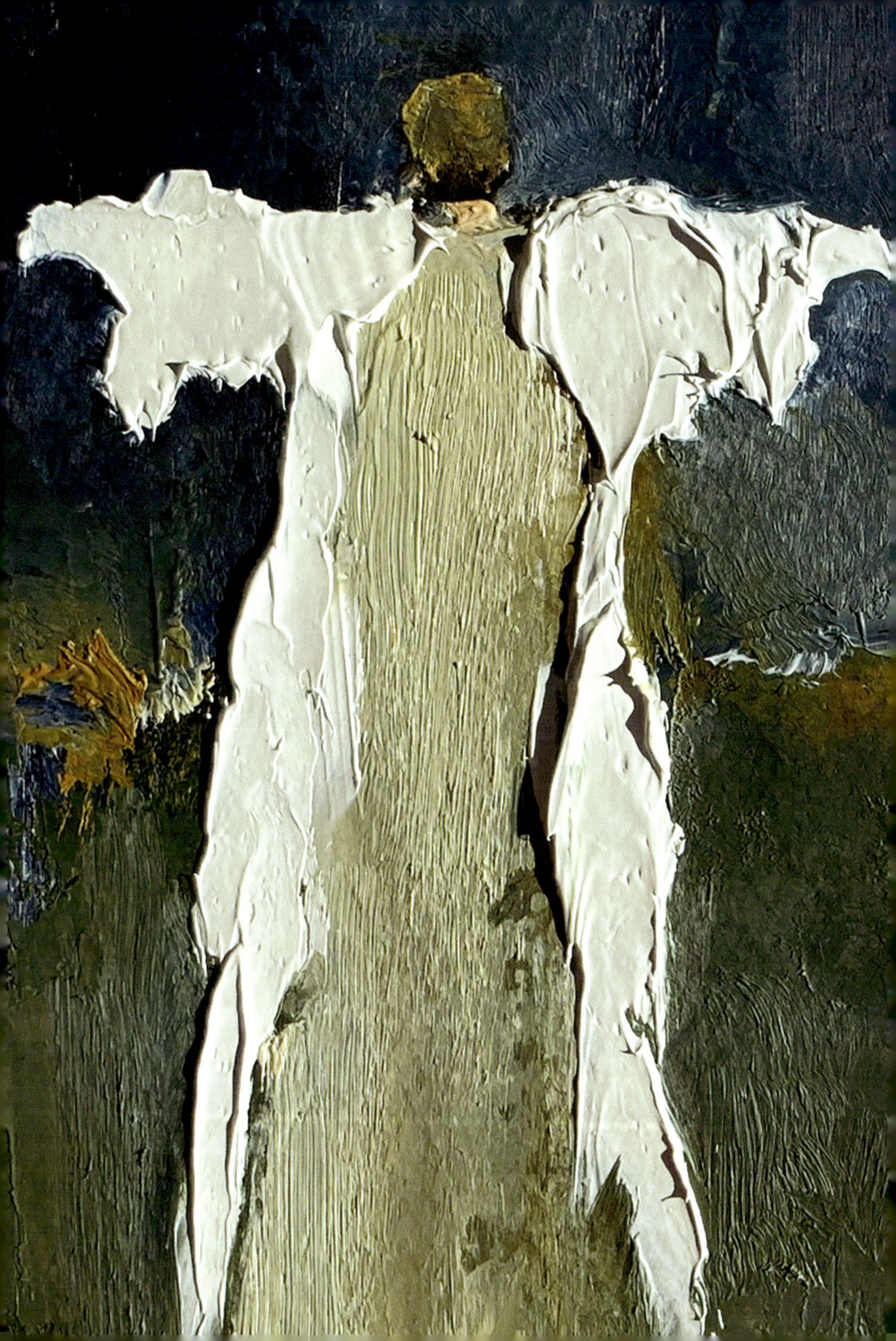

DAY 13

No Greater Love

"Greater love has no one than this: to lay down one's life for one's friends."

JOHN 15:13

My studio in Charlotte, North Carolina, is where I do most of my work. One Friday afternoon around five, a lady showed up with two homemade apple pies. Those of us in the office called her the "Apple Pie Lady" for years after that.

When she first arrived, it wasn't the aroma of the apple pies that got our attention—it was the fact that she had driven four hours to deliver them along with an apology for an abrupt email she had sent. You see, we had messed up shipping out her order, and in her initial anger, she sent an email she later regretted—so much so that she wanted to apologize in person. If I had been in her shoes, I would have been very upset, maybe even would have written that same email. But I wouldn't have gone the extra mile to make things right. The Apple Pie Lady drove a total of eight hours round trip to deliver a message of love despite the situation being our mistake.

I think about how we show love toward others a lot, especially during a season of busy, busy, busy. December is packed full of planning, preparing, cooking, wrapping, hosting, and shopping. It can be so difficult to look outward, but I know I need to redirect my focus during this busy season. I need to turn my heart toward others.

GO THE EXTRA MILE.

I encourage you today to think about the loved ones in your life or a distant friend who might need some extra encouragement. Make the time to go the extra mile for someone you love. What might that look like? Would it look like calling a friend and setting up a coffee date? Making a favorite dessert to share? Or showing up to a friend's house to simply sit and pray?

We all need extra encouragement and gestures of love, especially during the craziness of the holidays. I'm going to set aside time to bake my famous chocolate chip cookies and deliver them to some people who need a little extra portion of love. I'll likely stick to deliveries in my neighborhood—even though Apple Pie Lady and her extra-mile effort hold a special place in my heart.

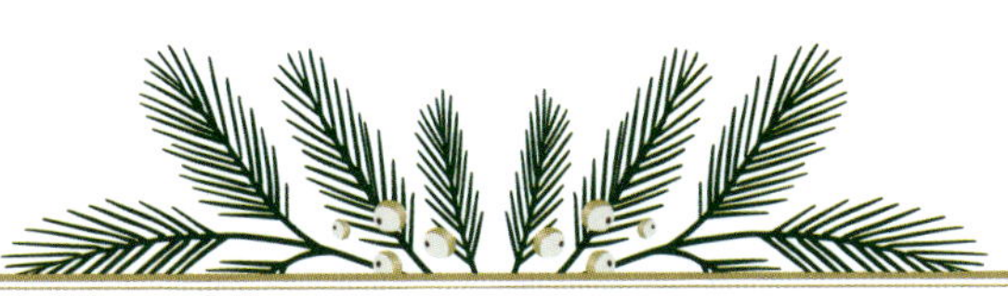

Dear precious Lord,

I'm not sure how far I would drive to apologize and ask for forgiveness, but I know how far You went to show me love. I want to pause right now, amid the busyness, to take in what You did for me, to reflect on how perfect Your plan was from the beginning. Lord, forgive me when I try to get ahead of Your plan. Forgive me when I am unkind or snippy with others. Fill me up with Your love and grace. I want to walk in Your ways today and always. Fix my eyes on Jesus, not only for this season but for the rest of my life.

In the name of Jesus,

Amen.

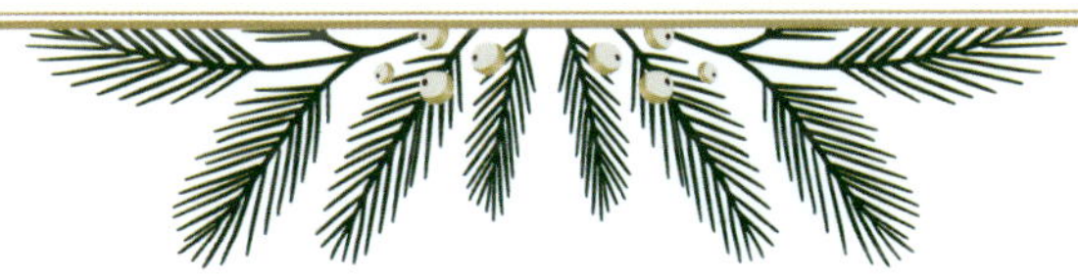

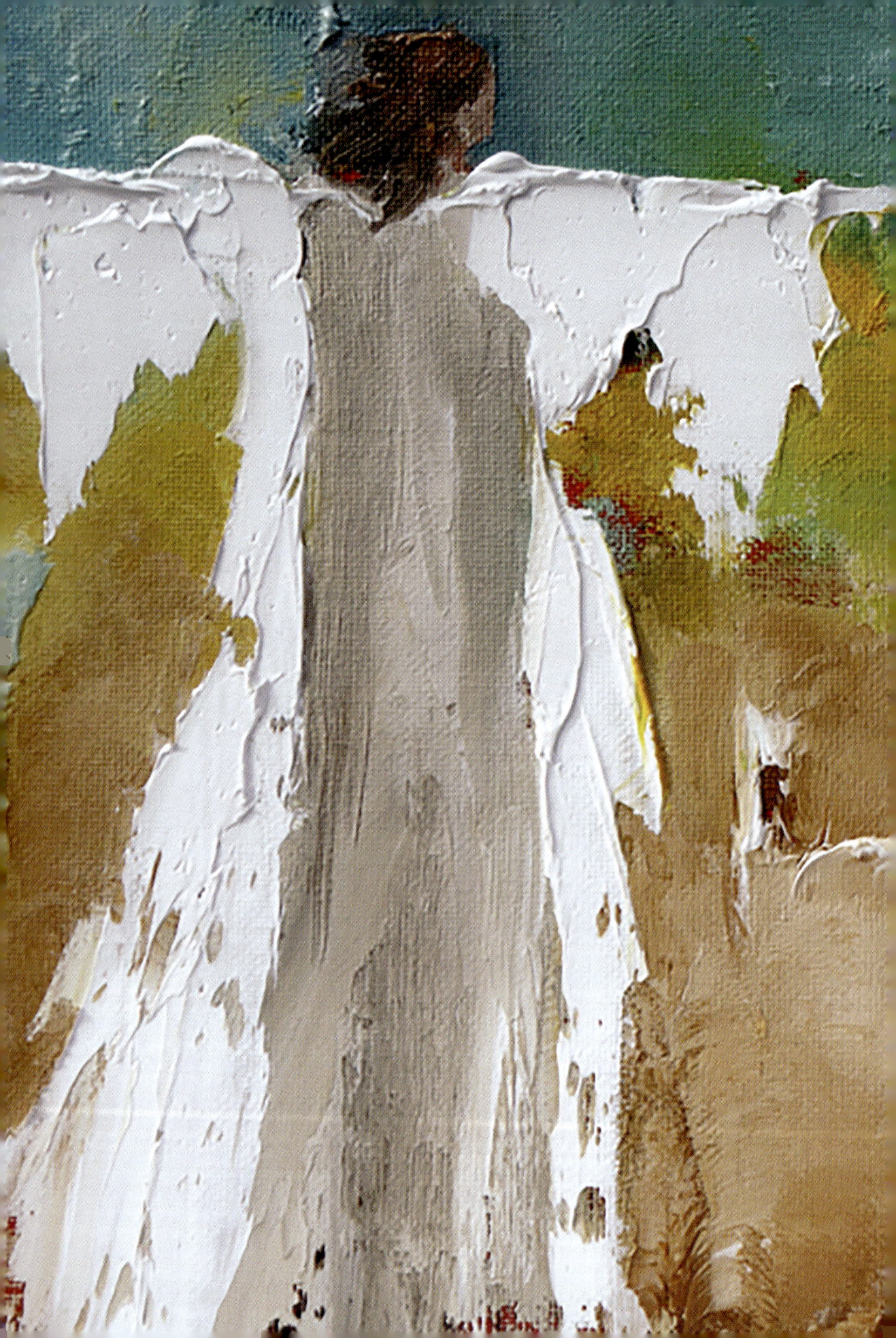

DAY 14

Love in Action

But God demonstrates his own love for us in this: While we were still sinners, Christ died for us.

Romans 5:8

As we approach Christmas, we find ourselves surrounded by the sights and sounds of the season—twinkling lights, festive music, and the joy of giving. Yet, amid the hustle and bustle, it's essential to pause and reflect on the true meaning of this time: love in action.

We are reminded that love is not just a feeling—it's an action. Love is service. The ultimate expression of love came when God sent His Son, Jesus, into the world. This act was not just about words or good intentions; it was a tangible demonstration of His love for all humanity.

Every day, and especially during this busy, festive time, we are called to mirror that love in our own lives. Love in action can take many forms: a warm meal for a neighbor, a listening ear for a friend in need, a simple smile to brighten someone's day, or forgiving someone who has wronged you. Each of these acts can be a reflection of the greater love that God has shown us.

God's love is the cornerstone of the Christmas story. The birth of Jesus is not just an event to celebrate but a profound demonstration of love that calls us to respond. In sending His Son, God showed us that love is sacrificial, selfless, and transformative. Jesus came to dwell among us, to understand our struggles, and ultimately to offer us redemption. His life was a living testament to love in action.

WE ARE INVITED TO CARRY THAT LOVE FORWARD.

During this season, we are invited to carry that love forward. Loving others is more than just a sentiment; it's a commitment to serve, to uplift, and to act.

As you pour out your love to friends and family time and time again over the next couple of weeks, know that your heavenly Father will do the same for you—you need only to look for it.

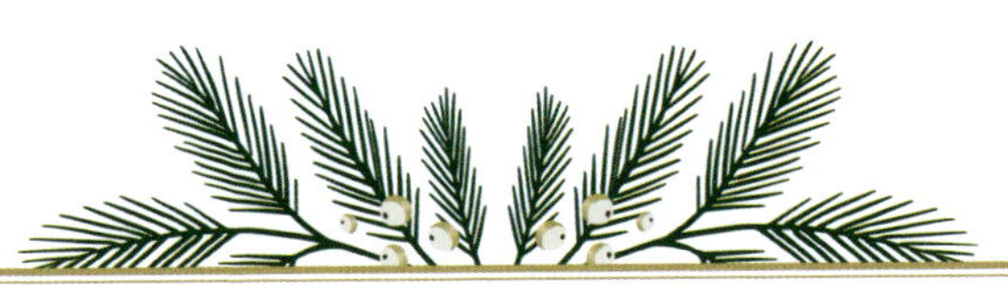

Lord,

Open my eyes today to see Your love all around me. I thank You for all the small moments of love and grace. I pray that I won't be numb to the patterns of this world that distract and confuse but that I will overflow with Your goodness and grace as I seek You each day. Today, show me moments of glory. Open the eyes of my heart to all You have for me.

In the name of Jesus,

Amen.

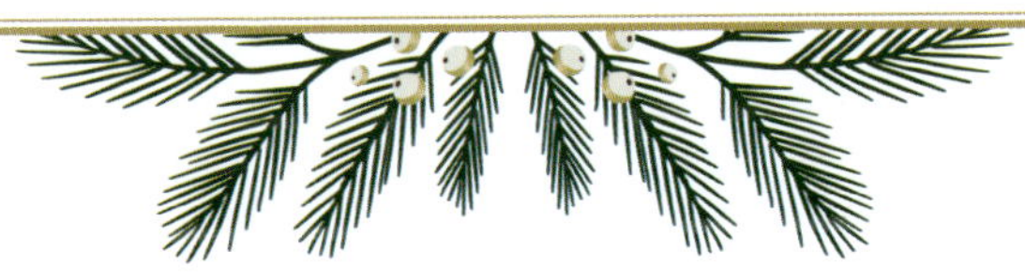

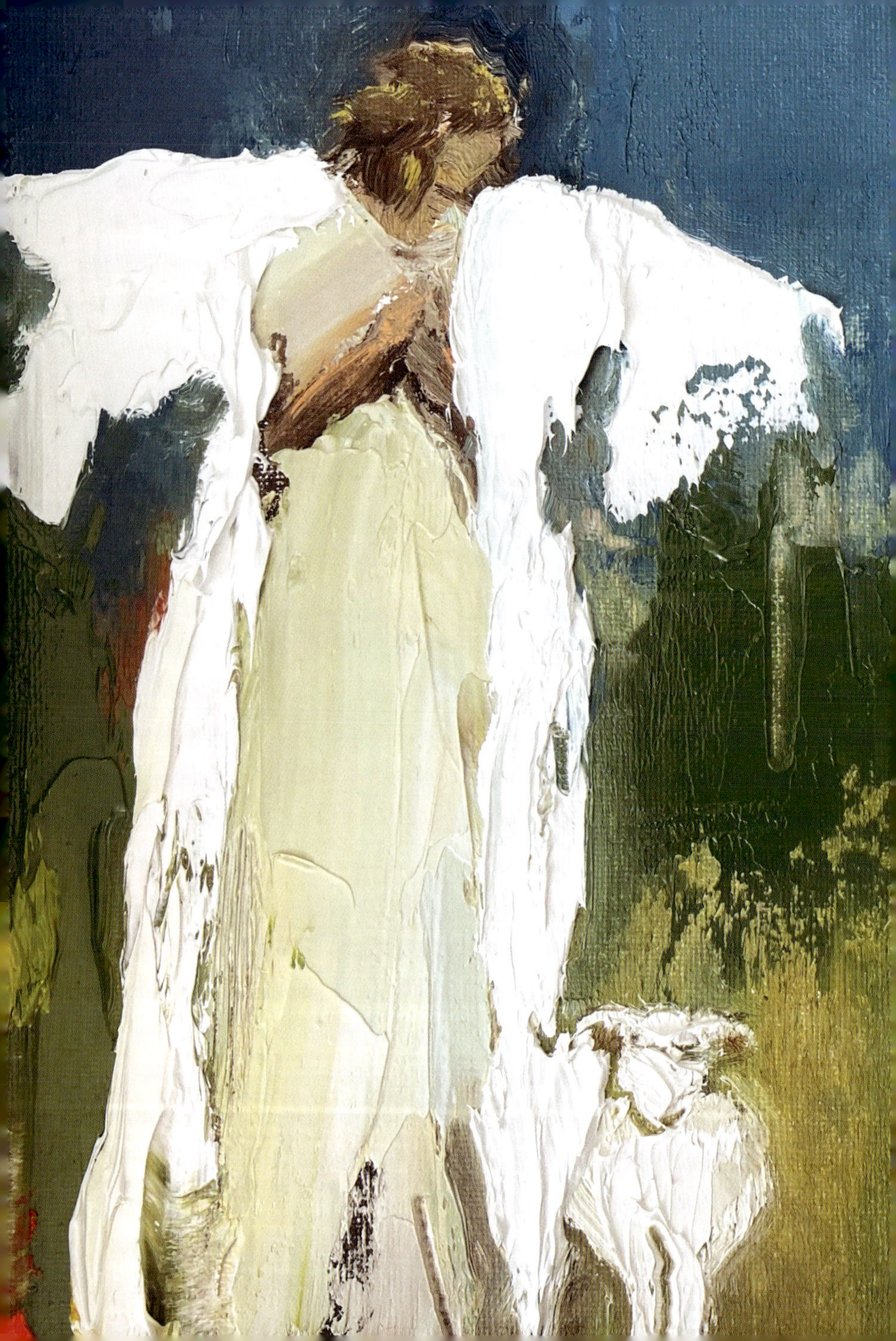

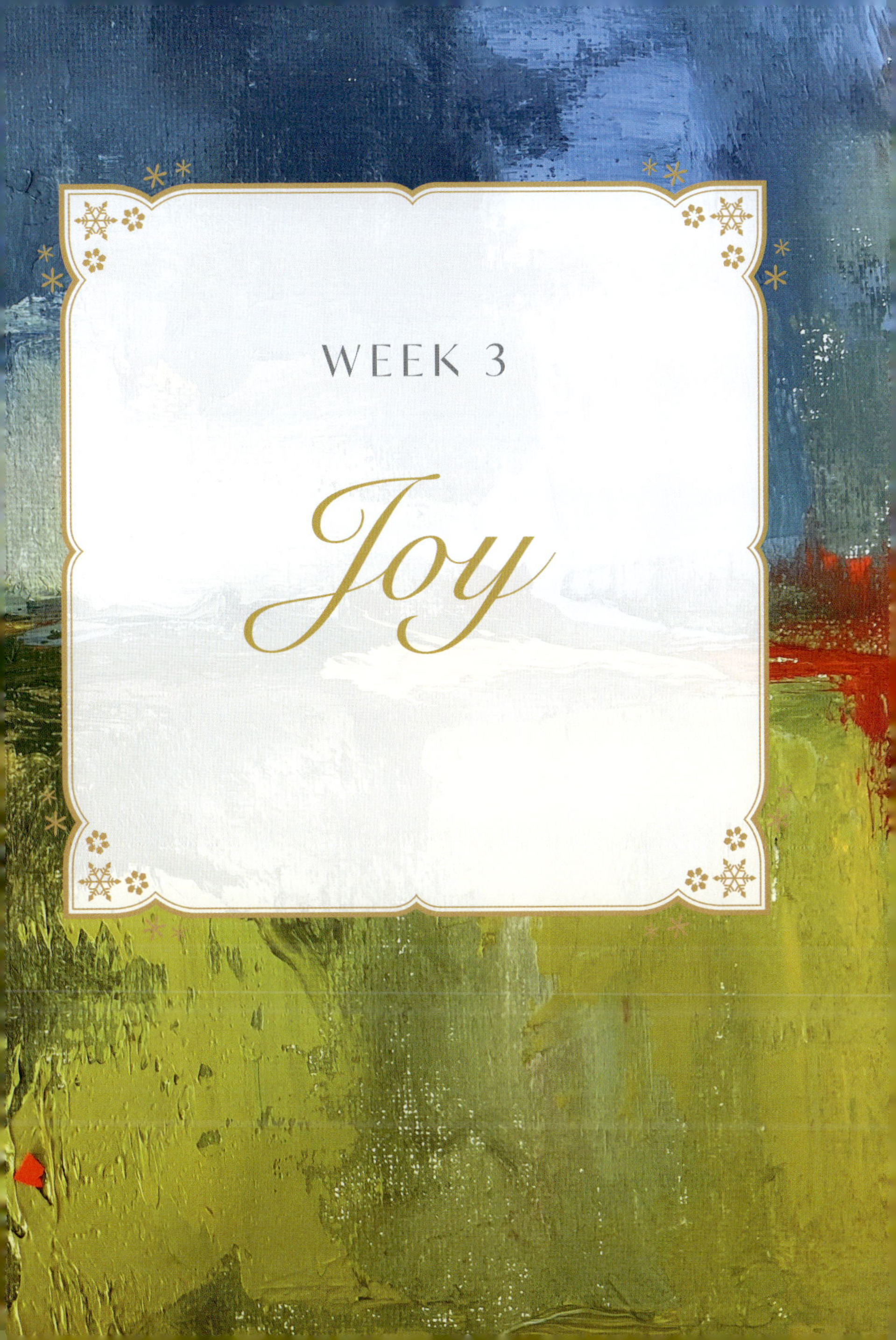

WEEK 3

Joy

The angels proclaimed *joy* to the earth . . .

Another night surrounded by a crowd of fluff and wool,
Another night of thankless vigilance, ignoring sleep's
sweet pull.
Another night camped out with a flock of bleating friends,
Another night spent wondering, *Is this my life until it ends?*

We lie down so tired, reclined and gazing up,
A murky sky so dark and black, like God's ink poured
from a cup.
"Just this once," one of our fellow herders says,
"something more,
"Something remarkable. I wish there was something else
in store."

And as though the sky took notice of his bleak and
hopeless words,
The clouds shift and build, the stars blink, and heaven
seems to stir.
A crack that feels like thunder reverberates through our
hearts,
And suddenly it feels as if our lives are poised and ready
to start.

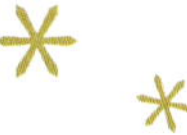

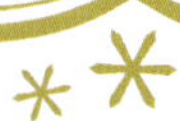

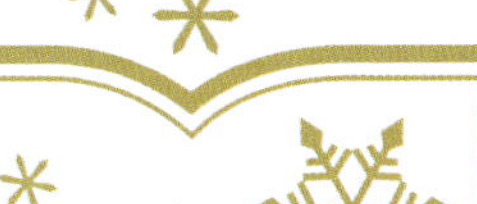

A lone star—a priceless jewel perched on a canvas
of velvet,
Draws our attention, though we can't pinpoint its meaning
just yet.
Then a voice commands our attention, urges that we have
no fear.
Is that—what's that?—a chorus of heavenly hosts has just
appeared!

Fervently they tell us of an arrival, a baby ushering in
divine hope.
The flocks around grow restless, the wanderers pulling at
their ropes.
They feel it too, the need to rush to the village and see.
Confusion falls away, replaced with unexpected urgency.

We approach with awe and wonder, surrounded by our
sheep.
We know this cooing bundle represents something profound
and deep.
Our spirits beckon to something greater as we gaze upon
the Boy.
Leaving behind the past, we embrace the promise of
hope and joy.

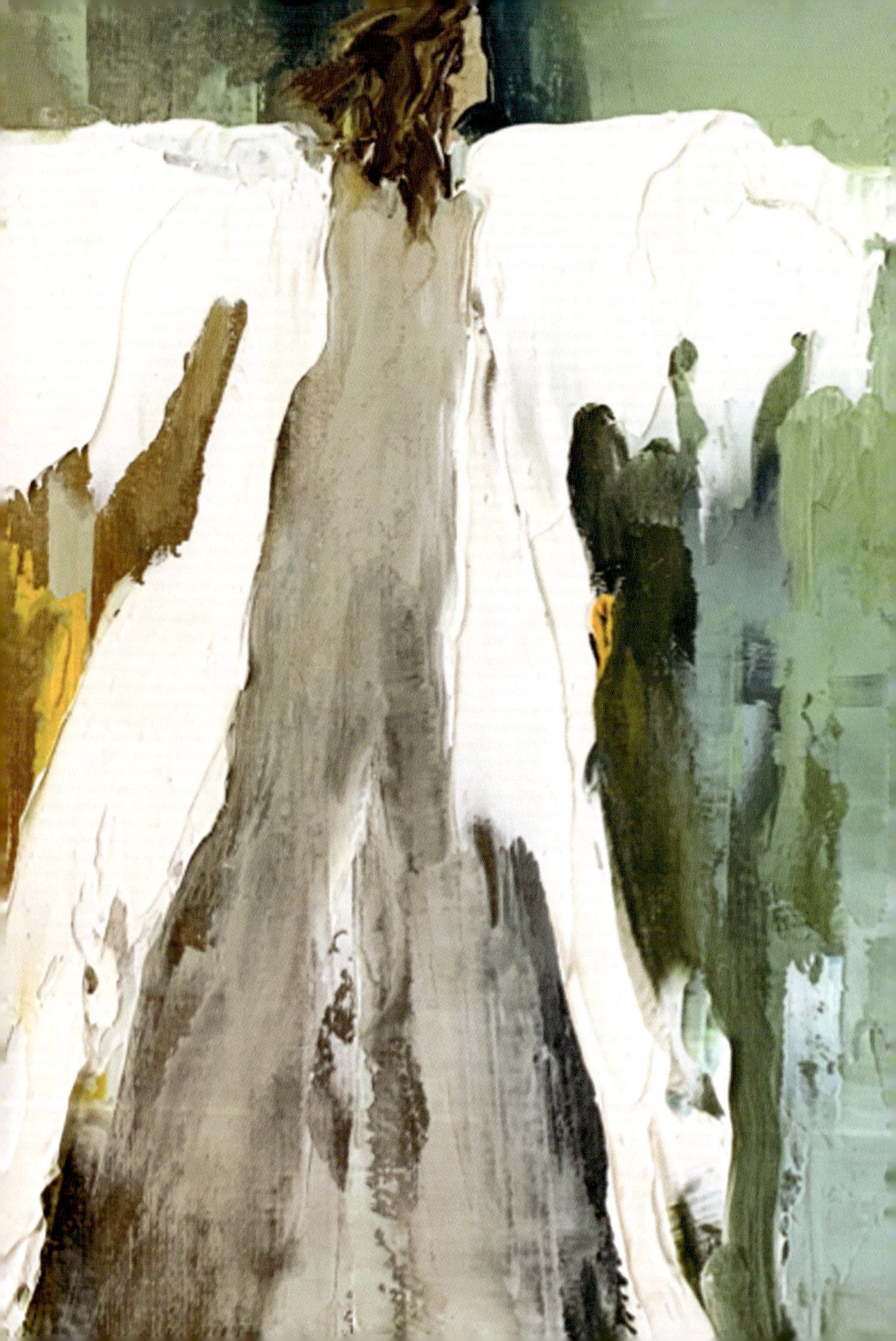

DAY 15

Good News of Great Joy

Splendor and majesty are before him;
strength and joy are in his place.

1 CHRONICLES 16:27 ESV

I think often about the shepherds in the quiet of that night, stars shining so bright overhead and only the bleating of the lambs to be heard. These weren't your typical shepherds out in the fields tending to regular sheep. These were rabbinical shepherds tending to special sheep—sheep that, when born, were wrapped in a special cloth to prevent them from getting any blemishes.[3] These sheep would one day be sacrificed for the sins of the people according to rabbinical law. Are you seeing the symbolism here?

The angels appeared to the shepherds and spoke of a baby being born and, like their sheep, wrapped in a similar cloth. This baby would one day be sacrificed for our sins, removing our debt once and for all. This is why we can rejoice with the shepherds when the angels say, "I bring you good news that will cause great joy for all the people" (Luke 2:10).

CONSIDER SPENDING SOME TIME IN PRAYER AND REFLECTING ON THE JOY JESUS BRINGS TO YOUR LIFE.

Sometimes I can't even get my head around this powerful news—that Jesus came to save us *once and for all*. There is no need to sacrifice animals for our sins because of a baby who was born that night.

As we approach Christmas Day, I pray that you would focus on the true meaning of Christmas. This holy day is not about presents, family gatherings, or yummy food, as wonderful as those things are. It is about God's perfect plan for an imperfect world, about a baby, the Messiah, who came to take away the sin and pain of the world. I don't know what's on your to-do list today, but consider spending some time in prayer and reflecting on the joy Jesus brings to your life.

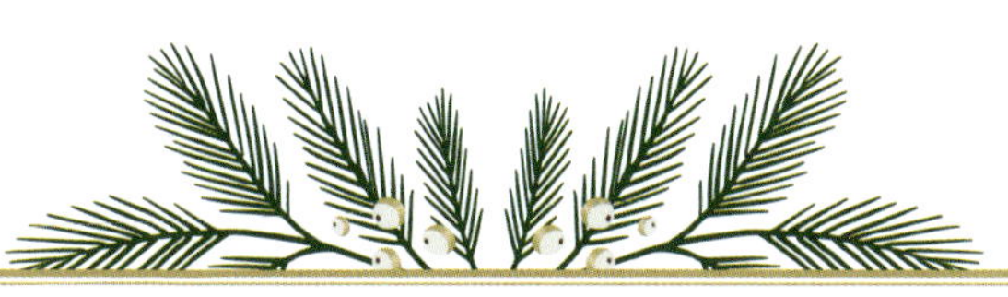

Dear precious Lord,

Fill me up with Your perfect joy today. Empty anything that is not pure joy from my life—like bitterness, anger, and unforgiveness. Help me to pour out anything that is not of You so that I am overflowing with joy. I cling to Your promises, and I am grateful for Your goodness and the joy that fills my life.

In the name of Jesus,

Amen.

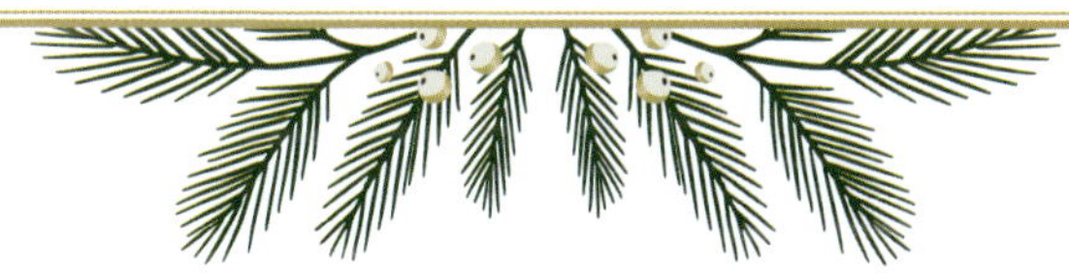

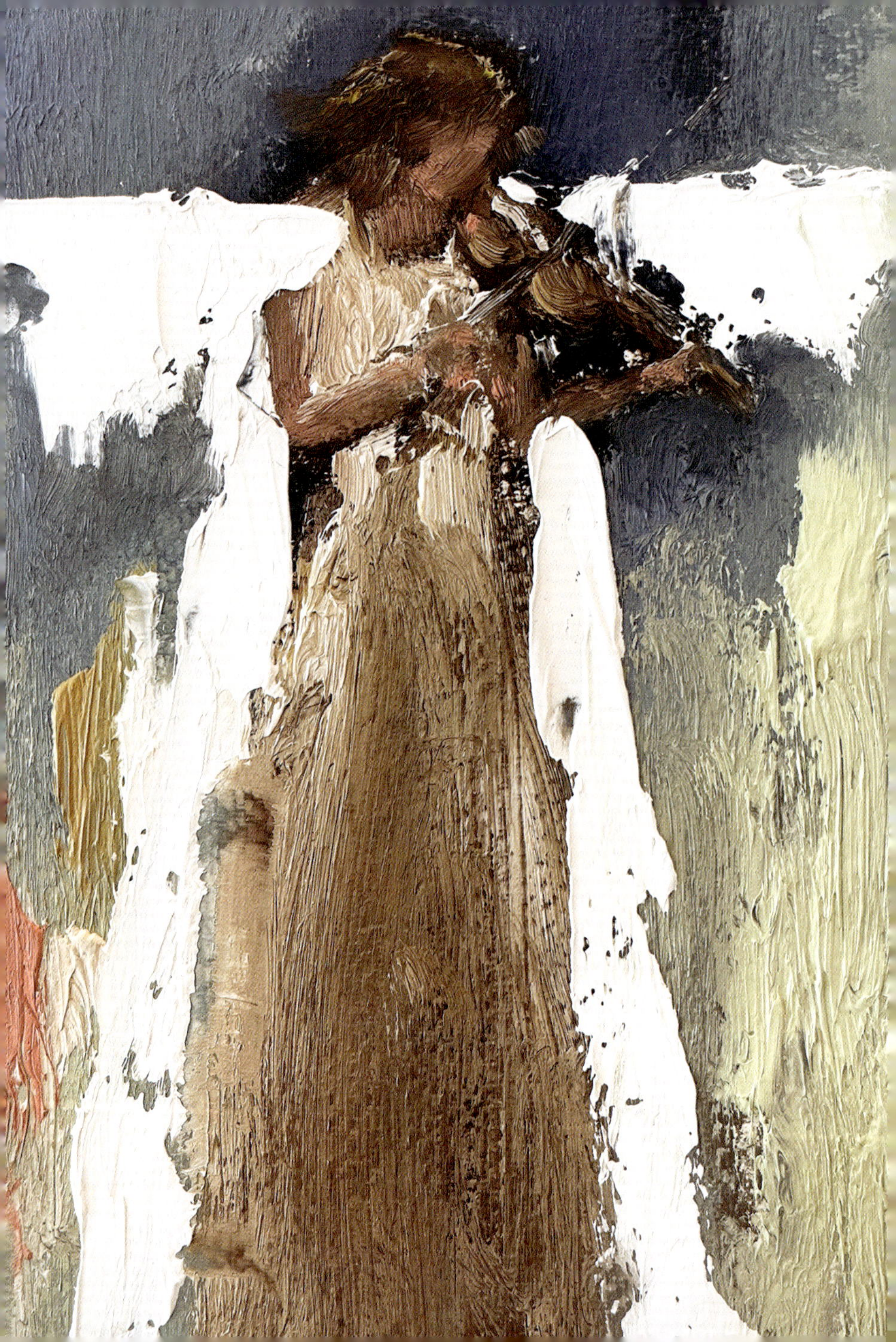

DAY 16

Come and Adore Him

Come, let us bow down in worship,
Let us kneel before the Lord *our Maker.*

Psalm 95:6

God specifically chose Bethlehem as the setting for His Son's birth, which required Joseph and Mary to make quite the trip to this village. They couldn't make lodging arrangements online or with a quick phone call. Instead, their journey's end was uncertain, ultimately landing them among hay in the company of barnyard animals.

Following the birth of Christ, the shepherds and wise men were instructed to follow a star to go and see the Son of God. For the shepherds, that meant abandoning their day-to-day duties and their woolly charges. For the magi, it meant traveling for nearly three years and escaping an evil king.

But despite the inconveniences and long journeys and lowly accommodations, much more was to be gained. When they saw the baby who was meant to rule heaven and earth, the magnificence of the Messiah made all hardships fade away.

COME ADORE HIM.

We live in a world of convenience. I have the entire Bible stored on an app on my phone. I have access to nearly any sermon thanks to the internet. There are dozens of churches in my hometown of Charlotte. I don't have to travel to get to Jesus. I don't have to fix my sights on a distant star and follow it wherever it goes. But perhaps that ease has also bred complacency. I don't always feel the urgency of Christmas.

My prayer for myself, for my family, and for you this season is that we would come adore Him, that we would travel in our hearts to the place where He's dwelling, that we would worship Him with the intensity and urgency the shepherds and wise men had. My prayer is that we would seek and find the joy of Jesus.

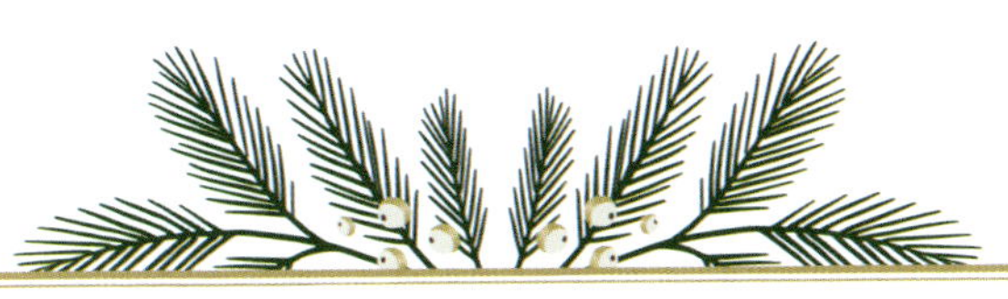

Lord,

I am grateful for all the conveniences of this life, but today, I pause and reflect on the night Jesus was born. The joy. The wonder. The sounds. The scene. Quiet my heart as You take me back to that holy night. O Lord, fill my heart with the joy the shepherds had seeing the baby, the joy Mary had holding her precious Son. Fill me until I am overflowing with Your perfect joy. Thank You for the miraculous gift of joy.

In the name of Jesus,

Amen.

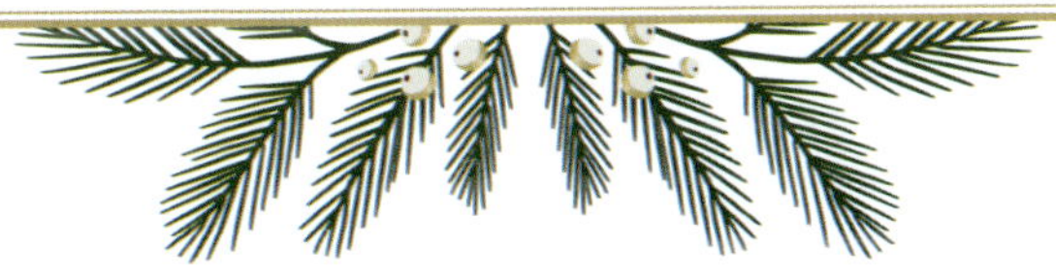

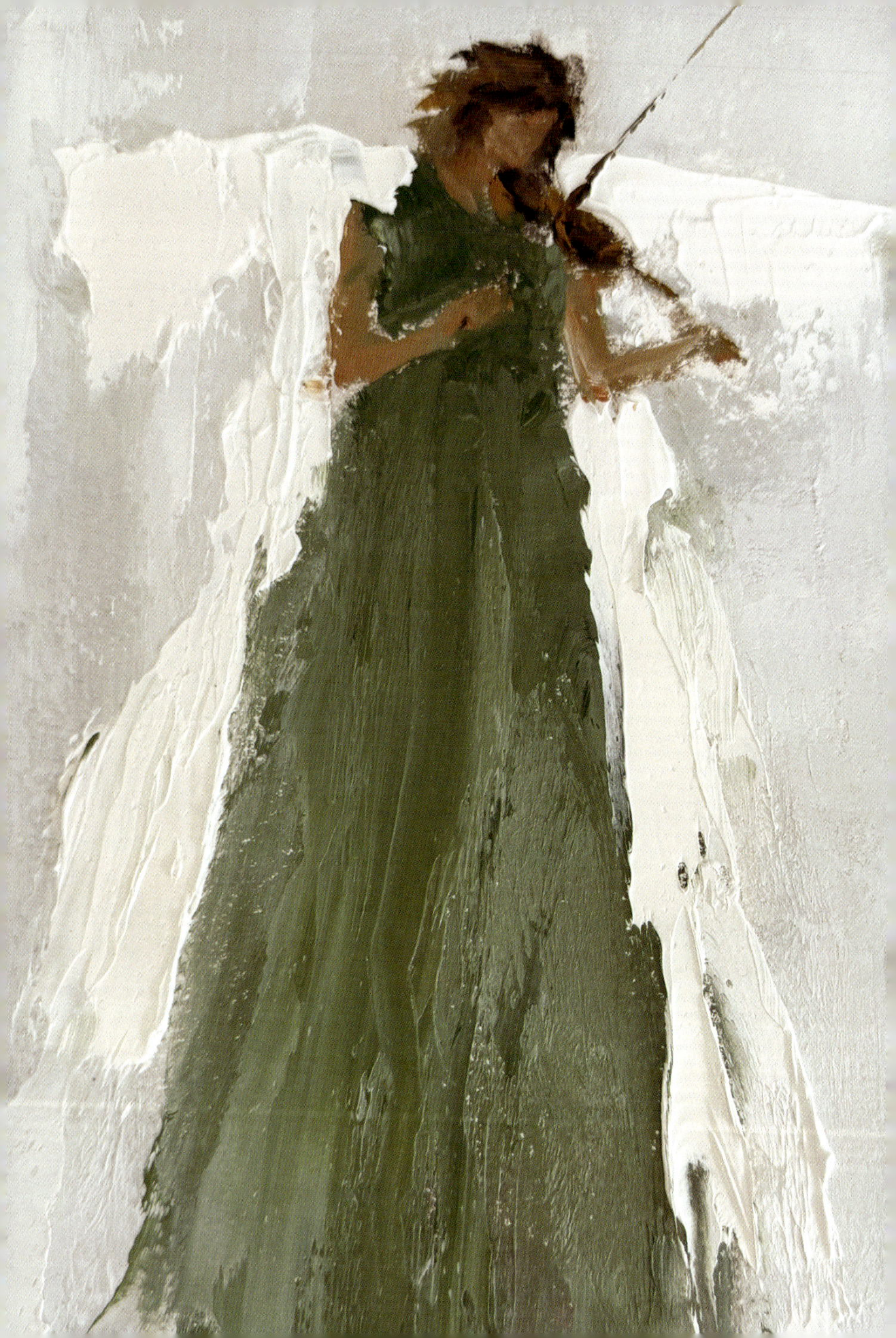

DAY 17

A Song of Praise

Make a joyful noise to the LORD, all the earth!

PSALM 100:1 ESV

Toward the end of his life, my dad had to wear hearing aids if he wanted to hear anything that was said. When he wasn't wearing his hearing aids, his world became quite silent. And with Parkinson's disease affecting his brain function, my sister and I had to navigate this new normal with him.

We realized that Daddy needed to listen to more music. When your world is silent, the brain functions differently. Research has shown that listening to music can reduce anxiety, blood pressure, and pain and can also improve sleep, mood, mental alertness, and memory.[4]

The Bible is full of references to music and singing. The apostle

Paul told us to teach one another "through psalms, hymns, and songs from the Spirit, singing to God with gratitude in your hearts" (Colossians 3:16). And in Ephesians we're told to make a "melody in your heart to the Lord" (5:19 NKJV). I cannot imagine what worship must be like in heaven. I only know that when I turn on my praise music and truly let the words sink deep into my soul, I feel the presence and power of God right beside me. So, while sitting at my dad's bedside, I've begun turning the worship music up. *It is well with my soul.*

LET GOD SPEAK THROUGH SONGS AND HYMNS.

If you're like me, you have probably been listening to the same favorite Christmas songs over and over this holiday. Today, I encourage you to prayerfully listen to the words of the music. Let God speak through songs and hymns that flow through your car radio or your home speakers. Sing to the Lord, praising Him continuously and making a melody in your heart!

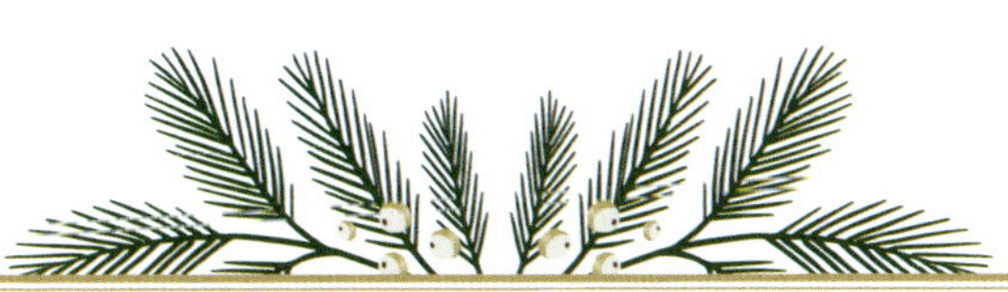

Precious Lord,

Today, I pray that You will speak to me through songs, hymns, and praise. I pray that everything I do today will be a joyful noise to Your ears. Through my words, my actions, and my thoughts, may everything be a song of praise to You. Open my ears to hear Your voice today. Silence the noise of the world and turn my thoughts to You and only You! I give You glory and anticipate with joy what this day will bring.

In the name of Jesus,

Amen.

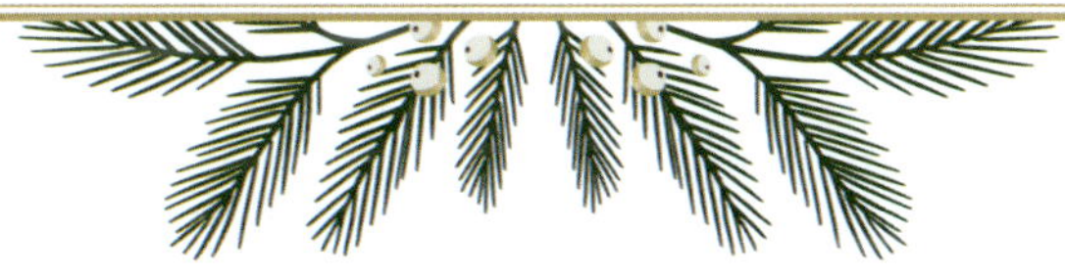

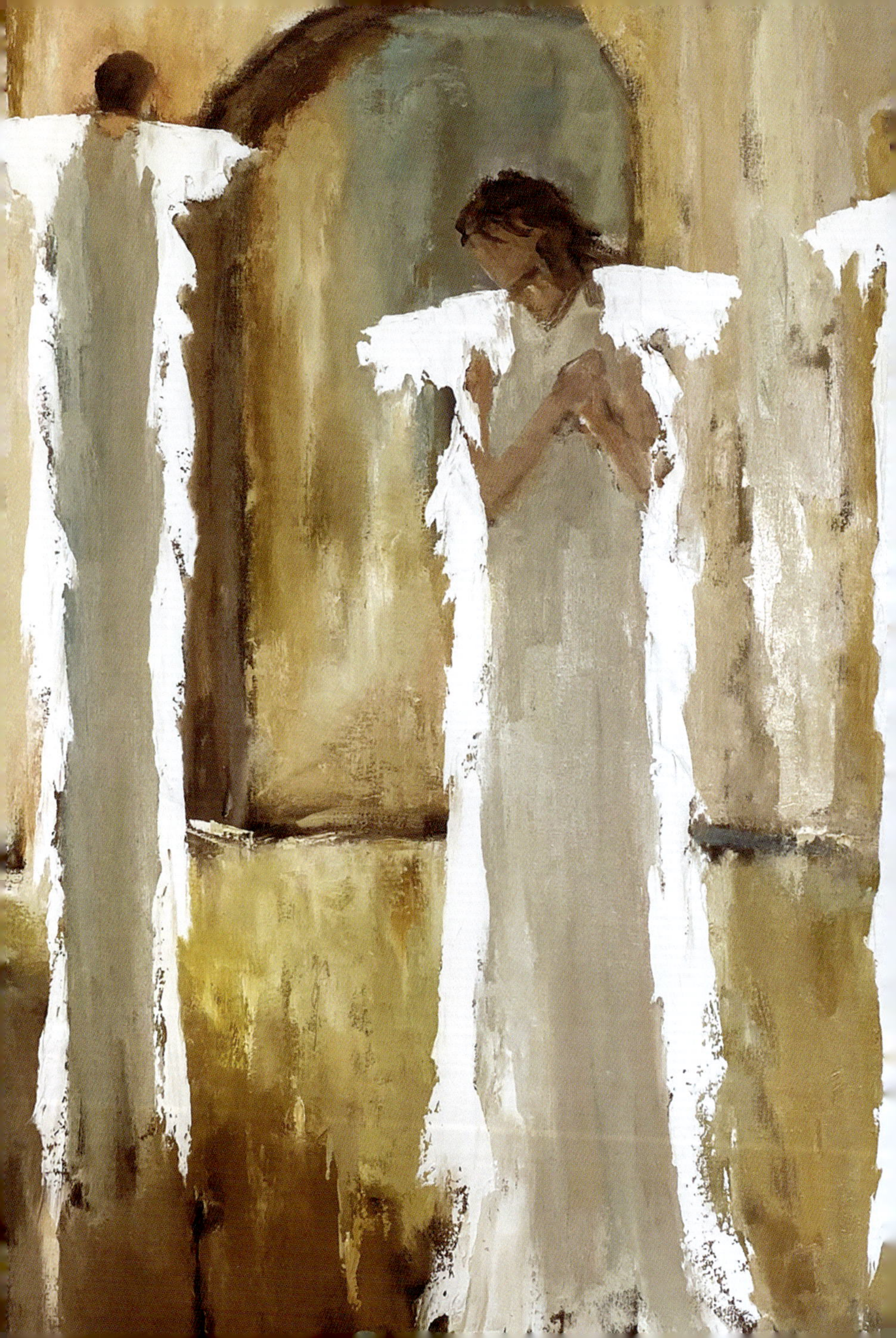

DAY 18

Joy Despite Trials

Consider it pure joy, my brothers and sisters, whenever you face trials of many kinds, because you know that the testing of your faith produces perseverance.

James 1:2–3

In many ways, Christmas really is the most wonderful time of the year. Along with the celebration of our Savior's birth, it's chock-full of family, traditions, food, parties, gifts, and good cheer. But with all that, sometimes Christmas can feel overwhelming. Frankly, it can be enough to drive a person crazy.

A few years ago, Christmas was a challenge for my spirit. I found myself losing my joy amid kids bickering, too many to-dos, and a calendar full of obligations. I was operating from an empty tank.

Several days after that Christmas, we hosted a party for some of our closest friends and neighbors. A team arrived to assemble a tent in our backyard—just in time for a huge downpour. And as if that weren't enough to send my anxiety over the edge, more rain was forecasted for the next day, the day of the party.

I walked under the rain-soaked tent to reflect on the holiday, and something inside me broke. I let my heart listen closely, and I heard God whispering, *Just surrender, Anne.* In that moment I repented for spending Christmas so focused on tasks and plans and keeping all the balls in the air that I had missed the entire meaning. My joy had been completely stripped away. I needed to place myself back in submission to the Lord, to reposition myself in a posture of surrender.

I THANKED GOD FOR RESTORING MY JOY.

During my time under the tent with God, I also snuck in a prayer, requesting no rain for the party. That evening, the clouds broke, and we enjoyed an oyster roast free of rain. I thanked God for restoring my joy and for giving us a rain-free night to enjoy.

It can be difficult to maintain a posture of surrender at the Lord's feet during such a busy and distracting time. But only by surrendering to Him and shedding our own plans and pride can we guide our homes, build our faith, and walk the path that God has planned for us.

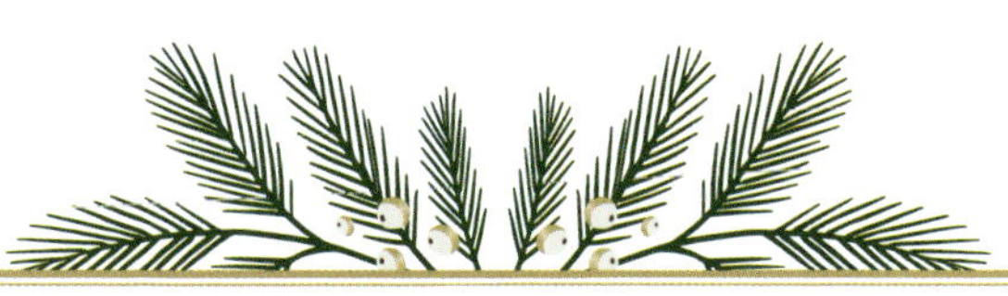

Dear Lord,

I come before You today and ask that You fill my heart with joy. I lay all my worries, fears, and tears at Your feet and know that You will wrap Your arms around me and carry me through. You will fill my heart with Your joy despite the trials I experience. Thank You that today, as I lay my head on Your shoulder, You whisper to my heart, "I will carry you through and fill you with joy. Trust Me, My child."

In the name of Jesus,

Amen.

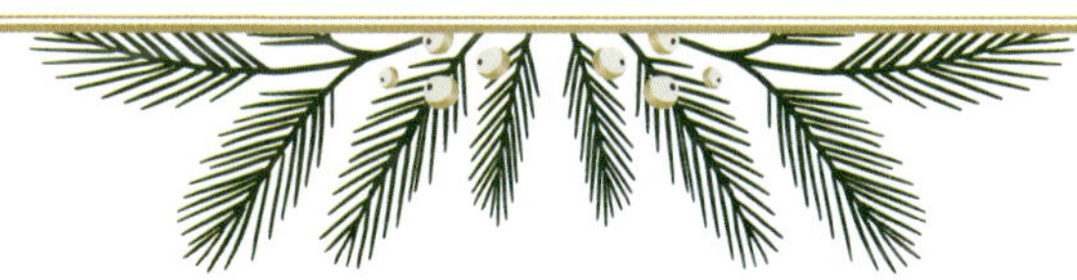

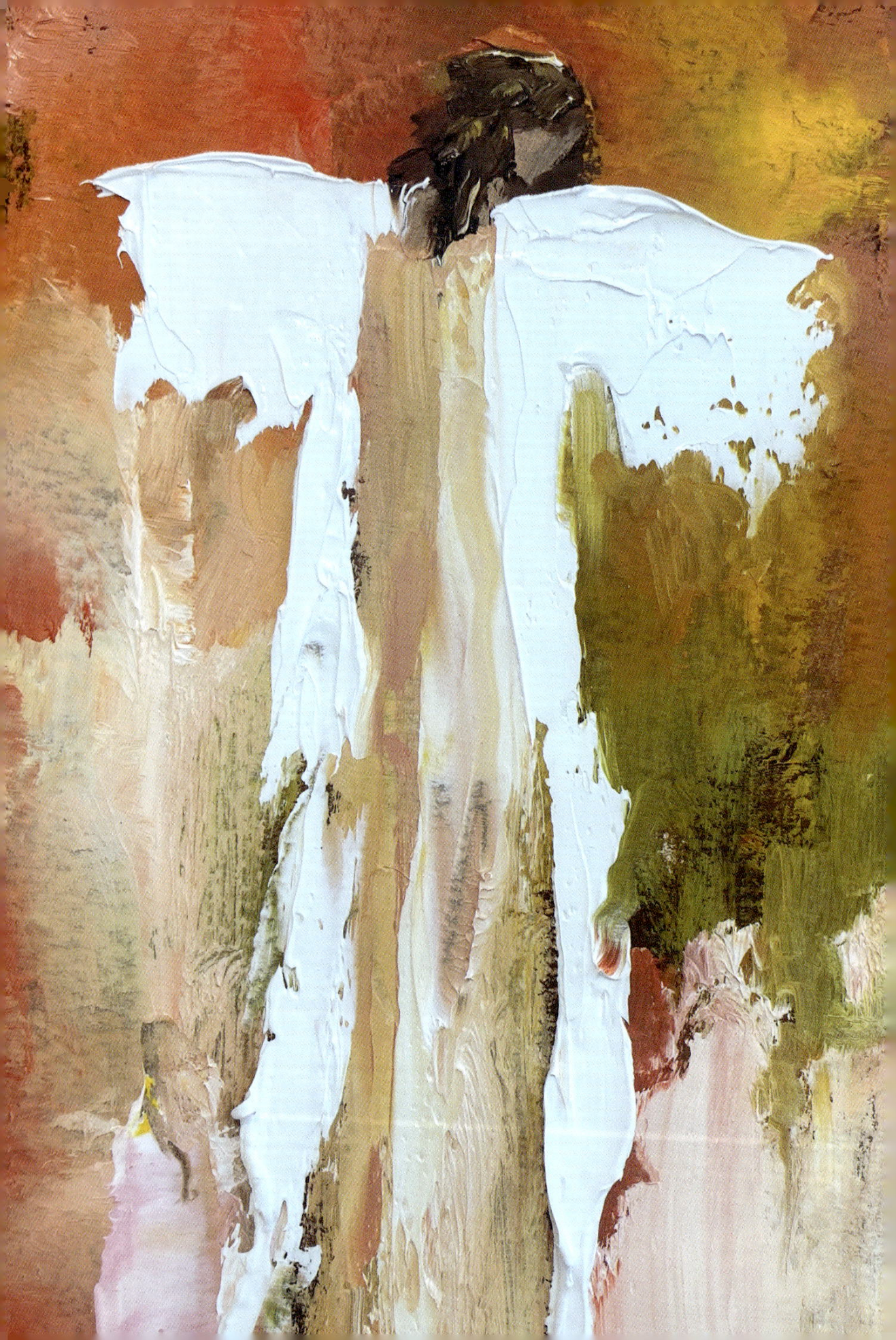

DAY 19

With Exceeding Joy

And behold, the star that they had seen when it rose went before them until it came to rest over the place where the child was. When they saw the star, they rejoiced exceedingly with great joy.

MATTHEW 2:9–10 ESV

We often think of the story of the wise men as one of rejoicing and adoration. And it is that. But what's often missed is that these men had been sent by King Herod with a lie—that he also wanted to worship this King of the Jews. But Herod's ultimate plan was to find the baby and end His life.

So the wise men traveled many miles, for several years, following a burning beacon leading them to the crib of the Messiah. And when they reached his home, they worshipped Him. They brought gifts and bowed before the prophesied King, standing alongside a baby who gave them every reason to rejoice.

Just before the wise men carried out their mission to alert Herod, an angel of the Lord warned them not to so that Herod couldn't carry out his evil plan. Can you imagine the shock the magi must have felt when they learned that the mission they had been sent on was a lie? And yet they had been given the opportunity to worship the newborn King—and to heed the angel's instruction so that He would be safe from King Herod.

KNEEL TOWARD BETHLEHEM AND SEIZE THE GREAT JOY THAT THE SAVIOR BRINGS.

In what ways can you recognize the Messiah as you go about your days in this season? Are you following the star, seeking Him out, searching for the King who takes away the sin of the world? Especially during Advent, when the weight of the world may feel heavy as we long for our Savior, we can take moments to encounter Jesus, who has the power to replace our cares with joy.

When you're overcome this season, kneel toward Bethlehem, even for just a moment, and seize the great joy that the Savior brings.

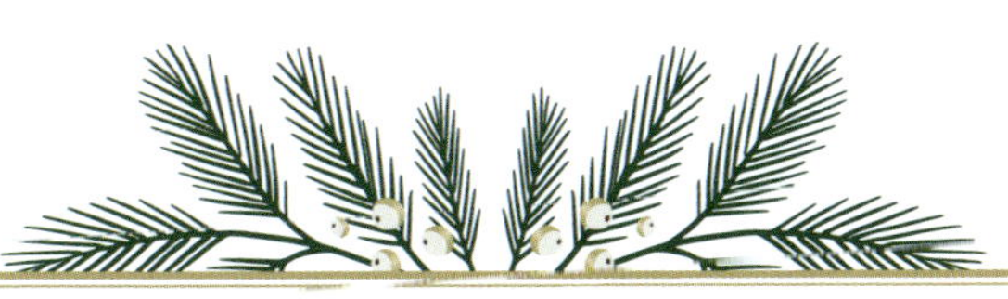

Dear Lord,

Fill me up with Your complete joy today. I cannot imagine traveling all those weary miles in search of the Savior of the world so many years ago, having my plans be interrupted, then turning and trusting. Today, I delight in the fact that You are my Savior and that You are right here with me. Even if my life gets interrupted suddenly, I can turn and trust You, rejoicing in all things today and forever!

In the name of Jesus,

Amen.

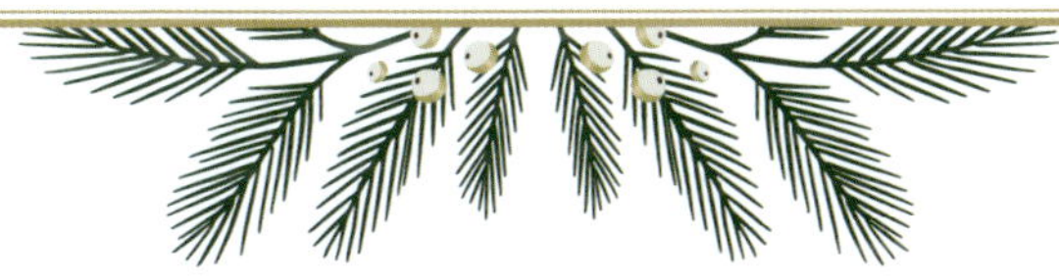

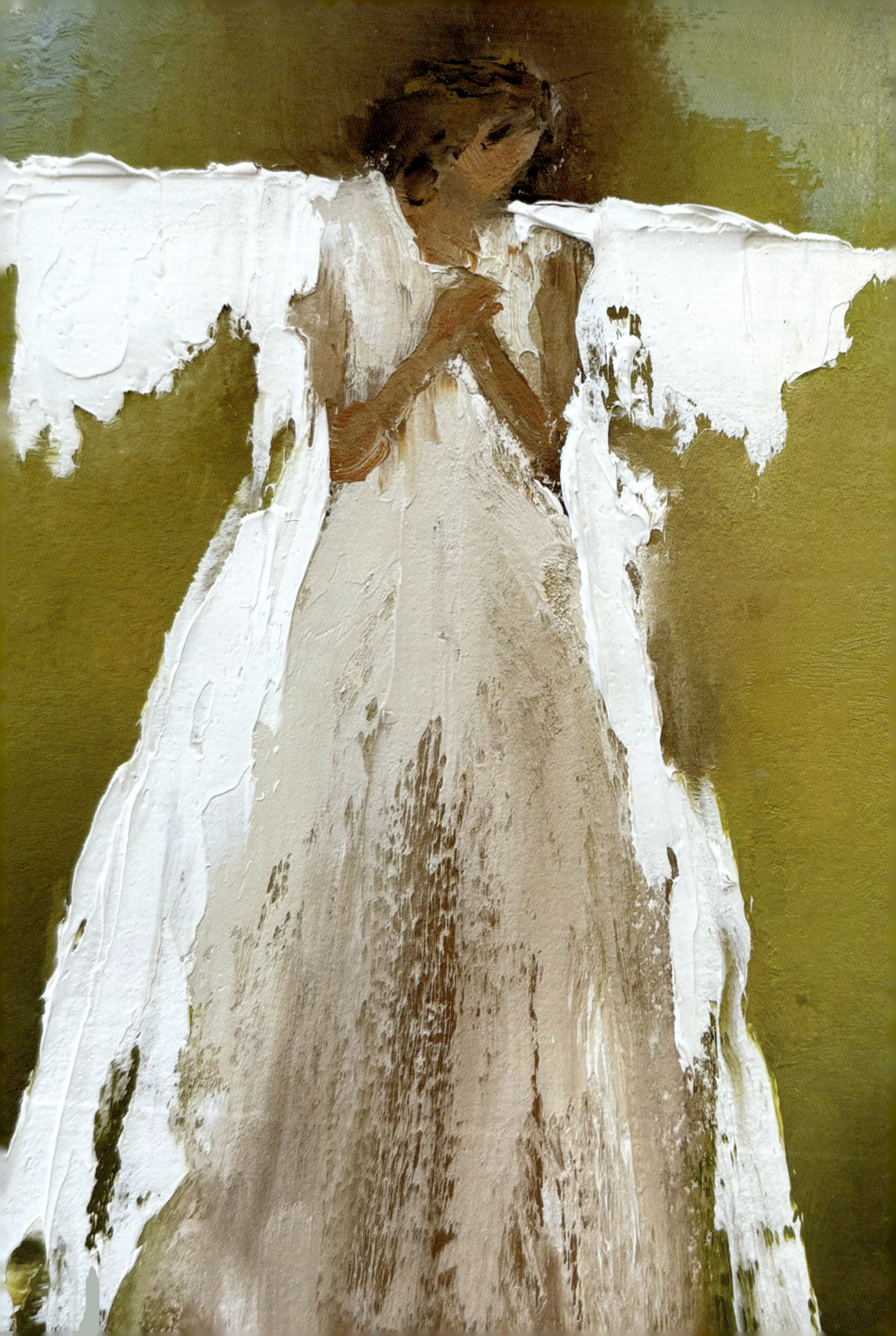

DAY 20

No Greater Plan

In those days Caesar Augustus issued a decree that a census should be taken of the entire Roman world. . . . And everyone went to their own town to register.

LUKE 2:1, 3

While I typically skim over the opening lines of Luke's account of Christ's birth to get to the "good" part of the story, I can't help but wonder what it meant for Mary and Joseph to be counted. They didn't really have a choice. A decree had been ordered, so they packed their bags, saddled their donkey, and traveled the miles required to be counted. Just an ordinary couple totaling a measly two in Caesar Augustus's count of people in the world.

Surely none of this was in Mary's plans. A year earlier, she hadn't anticipated carrying the Son of God. And she surely hadn't planned on having to participate in a census and then giving birth in a stable. But God wasn't concerned about a census counting Mary and Joseph.

He knew that His faithful servants had a role to play that far surpassed a census law. He knew in His grand design that they were not merely being counted, but counted *on* by all of humanity.

GOD IS SMILING BECAUSE YOU ARE MORE THAN JUST A NUMBER.

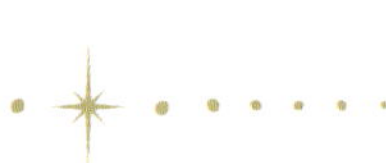

Maybe you're astride a donkey now, heading down a road to a place you never fathomed for your future. Maybe you're laboring inside a stable that feels too cold, too desolate, too wrong for the size of the promise you thought was being delivered to you. Maybe you're feeling like a nameless number in a crowd.

You may not be carrying the Savior in your womb, but the future God has laid out before you is greater than you could plan or imagine on your own. Maybe your Bethlehem—the place where you need to encounter Jesus—is waiting at the end of the road you're currently on. God is smiling because you are more than just a number. You matter to Him, and you can count on Him.

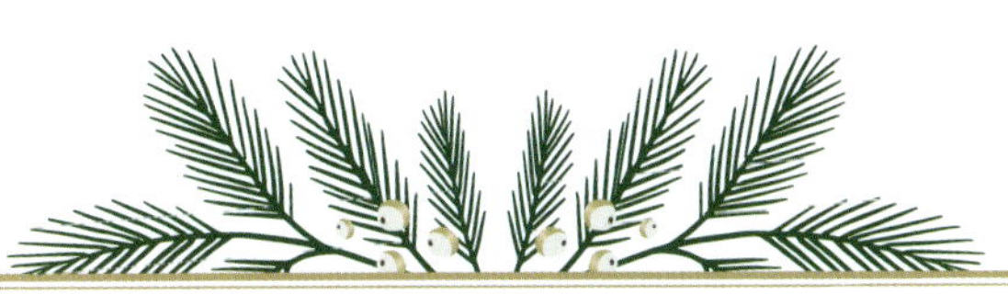

Dear Lord,

I just want to give You thanks for all that You have done for me. Help me to remember Your faithfulness and to trust in You for my future. My heart rejoices with gratitude, knowing that You will go before me, that You will carry me, that You will show me the way to go. I glory in Your unfailing love that brings me great joy!

In the name of Jesus,

Amen.

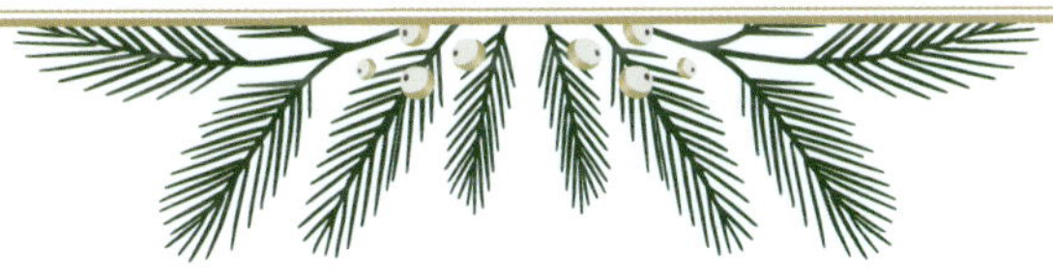

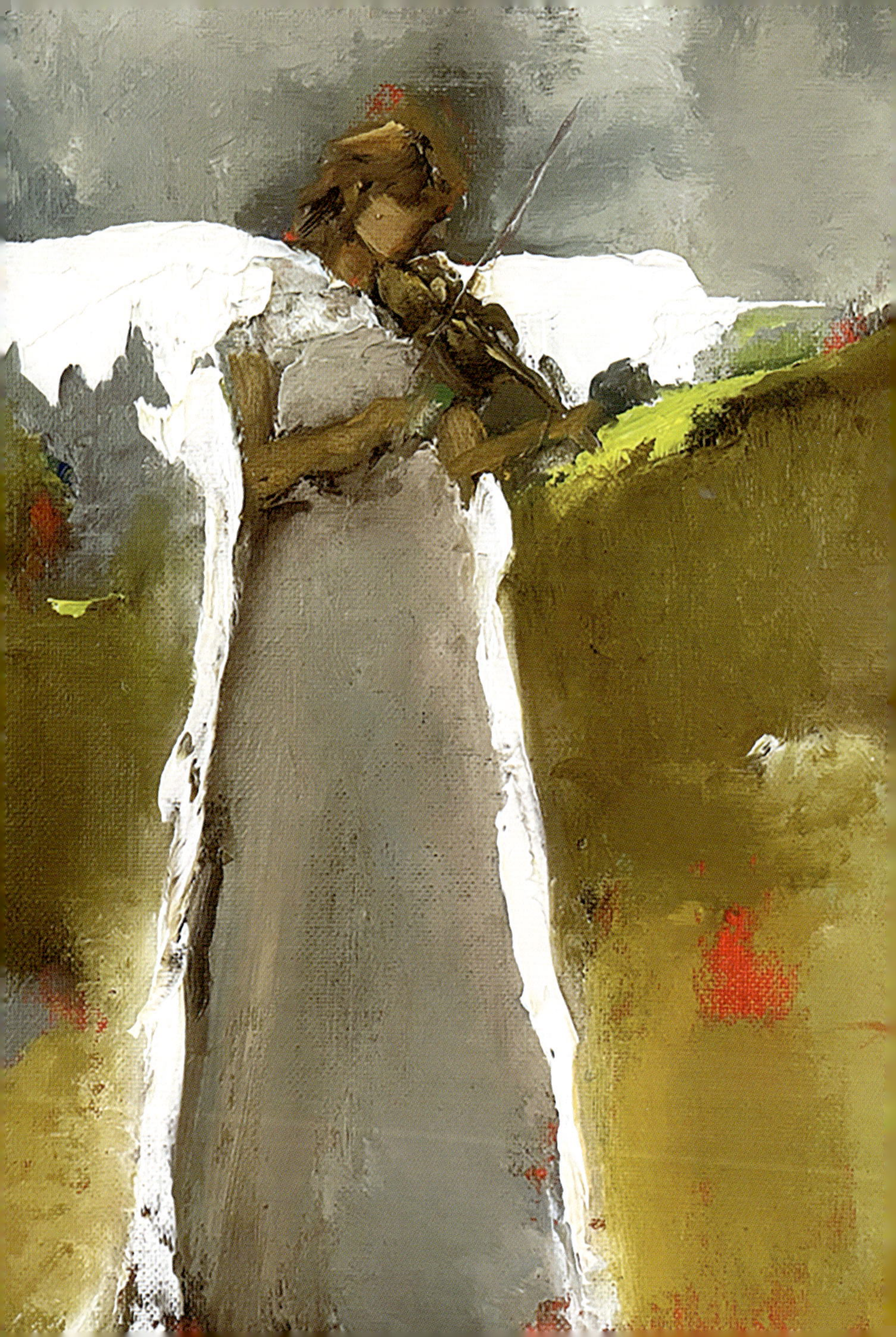

DAY 21

Create in Me a Clean Heart

Create in me a pure heart, O God, and renew a steadfast spirit within me.

PSALM 51:10

In the familiar song "Joy to the World," my favorite line is "Let ev'ry heart prepare Him room."[5] Have you prepared room in your heart for Jesus this season? And not just *parts* of your heart—your *entire* heart? Have you cleaned out the stuff that hinders you from letting Him in?

I love the analogy of a junk drawer. I'm sure you have one somewhere in your house—a drawer that continually collects the odds and ends of your home. Mine contains a single key that no one knows what it belongs to, a fountain pen almost out of ink, and pennies and coins scattered throughout. I spend countless minutes sorting, cleaning, and throwing away the unnecessary items that accumulate in this drawer, yet within a few days, it's somehow full and messy again.

Our hearts can be like that. When we do not consistently sort through the mess that builds up, removing the junk we don't want to deal with, it hinders our relationship with Jesus. Things like unforgiveness, anger, laziness—they clutter up the precious space in our hearts that could be filled with love and joy.

HE SEES ALL OF OUR BROKENNESS, ALL OF OUR PAIN . . . AND HE COMES TO HEAL OUR HEARTS.

I pray that today you would spend some time asking Jesus to clean out the junk drawer of your heart. Prepare room in your heart for Him to work miracles in your life. All He asks is that we come to Him. He sees all of our brokenness, all of our pain, and all of our junk—and He comes to heal our hearts. That is something to rejoice in this Advent season.

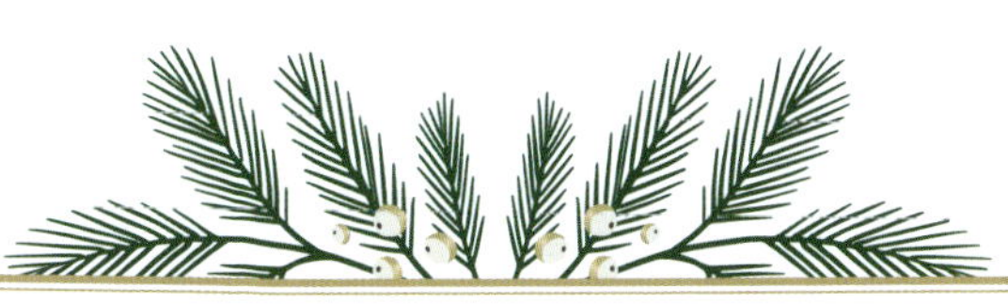

Dear Lord,

Create in me a clean heart. Dig up anything that would hinder the light of Jesus from shining through my life. As I sit still in Your presence, reveal anything that needs to be left at the foot of the cross. If there is any anger, any unforgiveness, anything that is not of You, please help me let go and cling to You and Your promises. I know that as You cleanse my heart, You will fill me to overflowing with Your perfect and complete joy this Christmas season.

In the name of Jesus,

Amen.

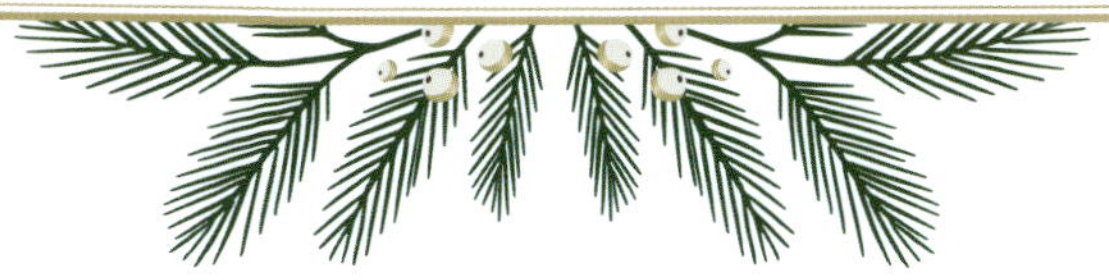

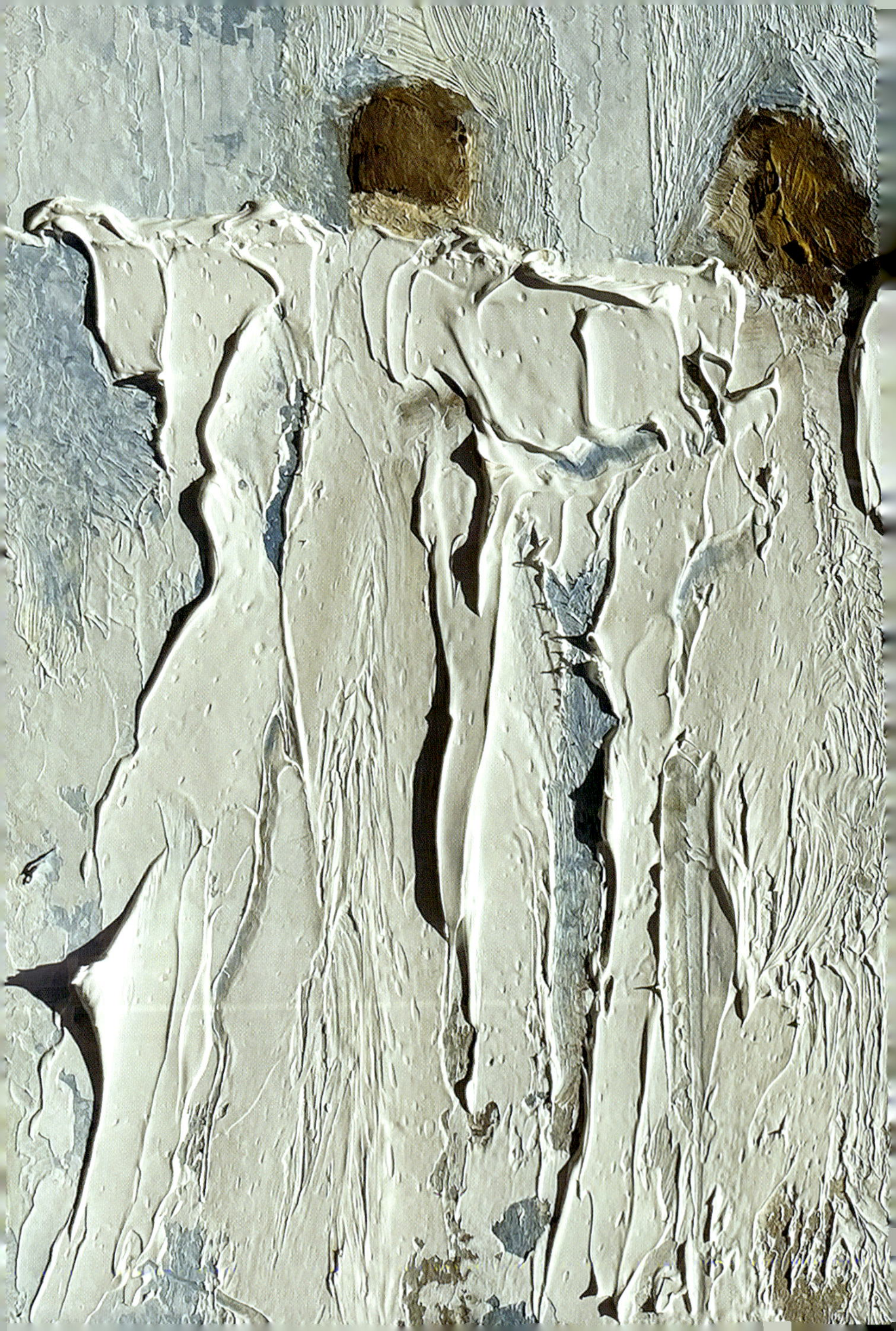

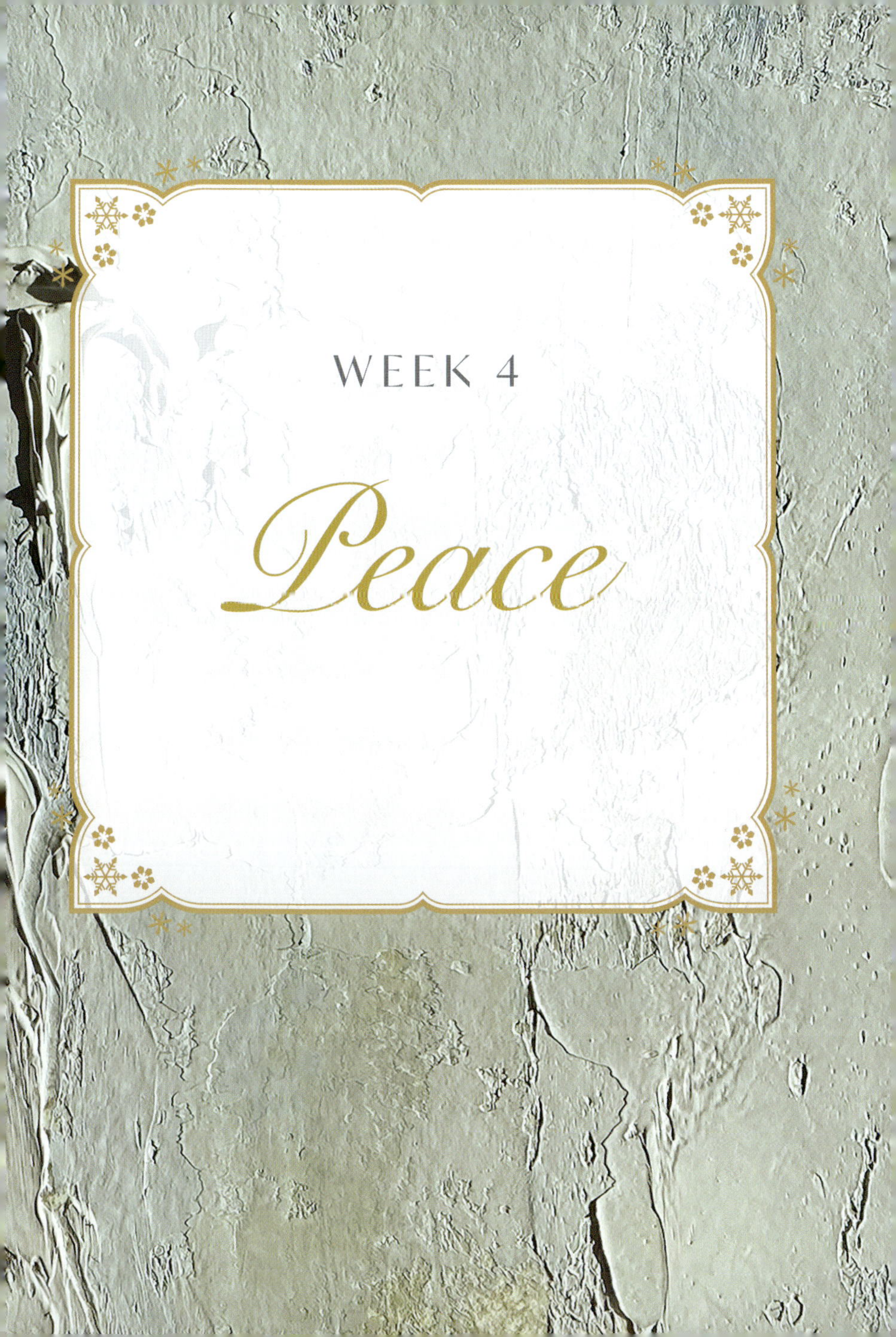

WEEK 4

Peace

The angels pronounced *peace* to all men . . .

In the hush of a winter's night so clear,
When stars twinkle brightly, drawing near,
A gentle calm settles over all,
As snow softly blankets the world so small.

Peace descends with a whispering sigh,
As angels above sing in the sky,
Their voices echoing through the land,
Spreading hope with a gentle hand.

In manger low, a baby lies,
Bringing light to the darkest skies,
His presence a gift of love so pure,
A promise of hope that will endure.

Let peace reign in every heart,
A bond that will never depart,
For in this season of joy and cheer,
May we hold on to peace, year after year.

So let us come together as one,
In the spirit of peace, until the day is done,
For Christmas brings a message so clear,
Of love, of hope, of peace so dear.

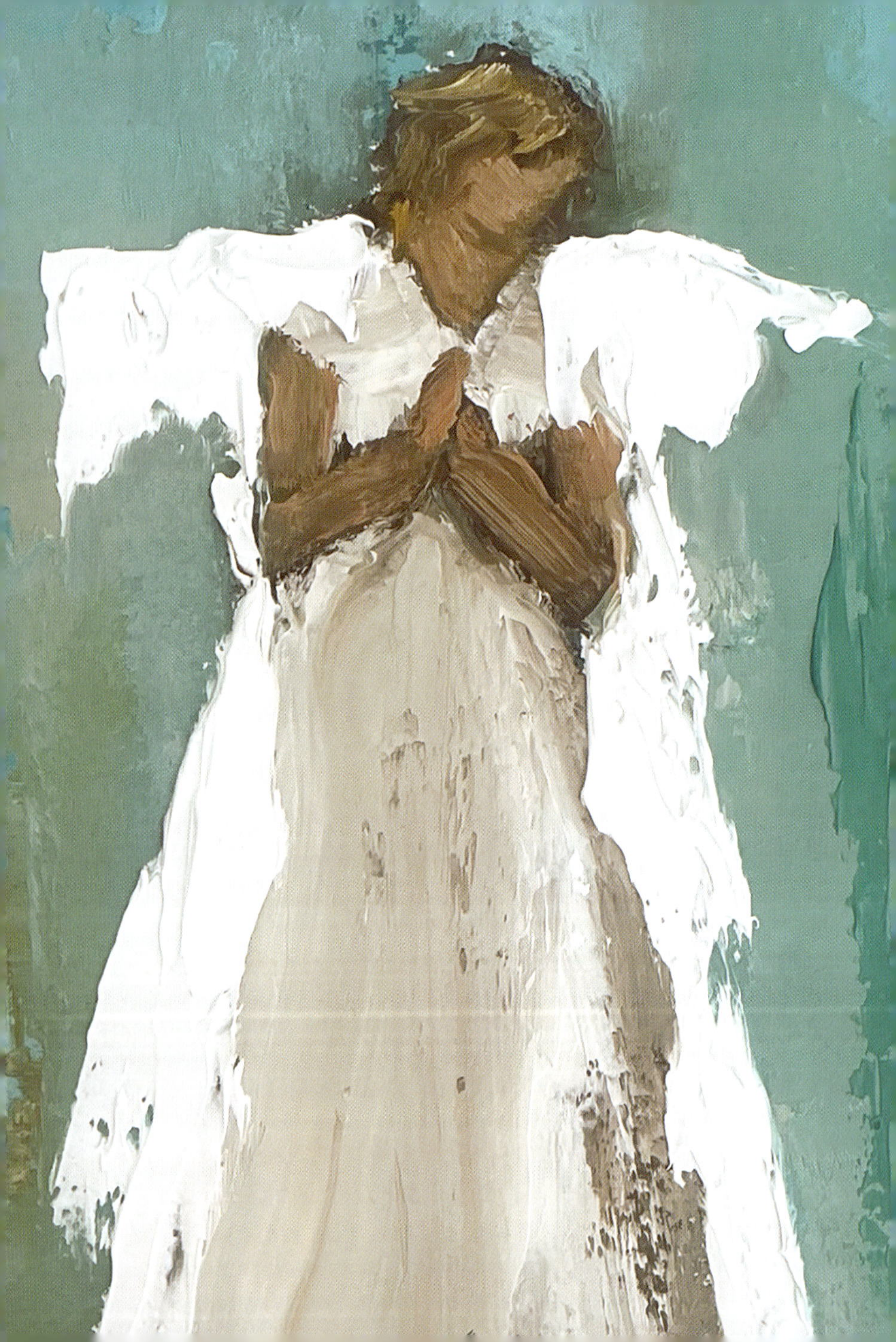

DAY 22

Be Still

For to us a child is born, to us a son is given, and the government will be on his shoulders. And he will be called Wonderful Counselor, Mighty God, Everlasting Father, Prince of Peace.

ISAIAH 9:6

I hope that over these past few weeks you have carved out some time where you could sit before the Lord and reflect on His goodness and glory during this season. We are now in week four of Advent, and our focus is on peace. Are you feeling peaceful right now?

If you are feeling overwhelmed because there are only a few more days left to finish your to-do list, I pray that you would pause right now and ask the Lord for His everlasting peace to surround you. Ask Him to fill you with His peace that passes all understanding. You don't want to miss that peace by continuing to rush around and dart from place to place.

"Be still, and know that I am God" (Psalm 46:10). He calls us to be still and know. To be still and listen. To be still and trust. The to-do lists will always be there and will continue to grow, but the opportunity to sit before the King of kings and the Lord of lords is waiting. He wants to bring your heart into a place of perfect peace despite the noise that gets louder and louder around you.

TRUST THAT THE PRINCE OF PEACE WILL SURROUND YOU THIS DAY AND THE DAYS AHEAD!

So today, I encourage you to turn off anything that might be distracting you from being still and knowing God. Tuck away your list, or better yet, surrender that list to Him and trust that the Prince of Peace will surround you this day and the days ahead!

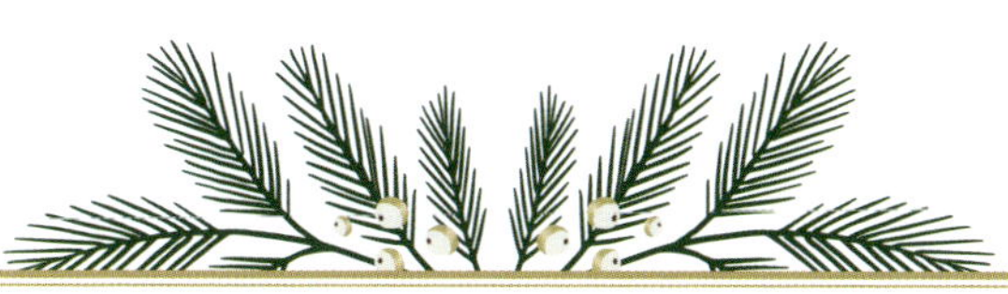

Dear Lord,

There are days when I am rushing around and forget to surrender all to You. I don't want to be in the fast lane that continuously rushes forward. I want to pause and feel Your loving presence surrounding me and bringing me peace in the midst of the chaos. Lord, direct my steps today to walk humbly with You and to surrender all the things on my to-do list to You. I thank You for all the little God moments today that bring peace to my heart, mind, body, and soul. I give You glory for this day and what it will bring.

In the name of Jesus,

Amen.

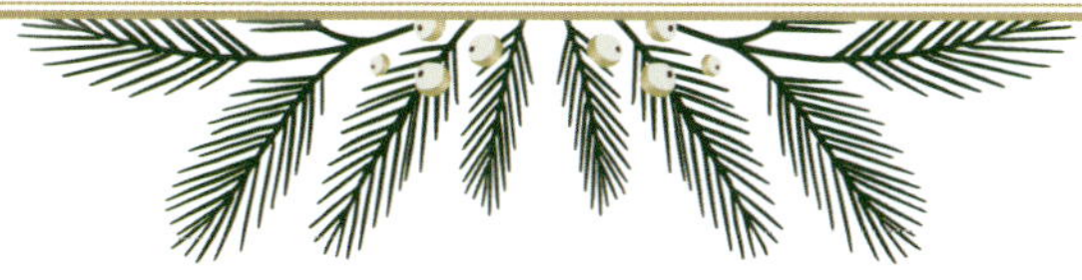

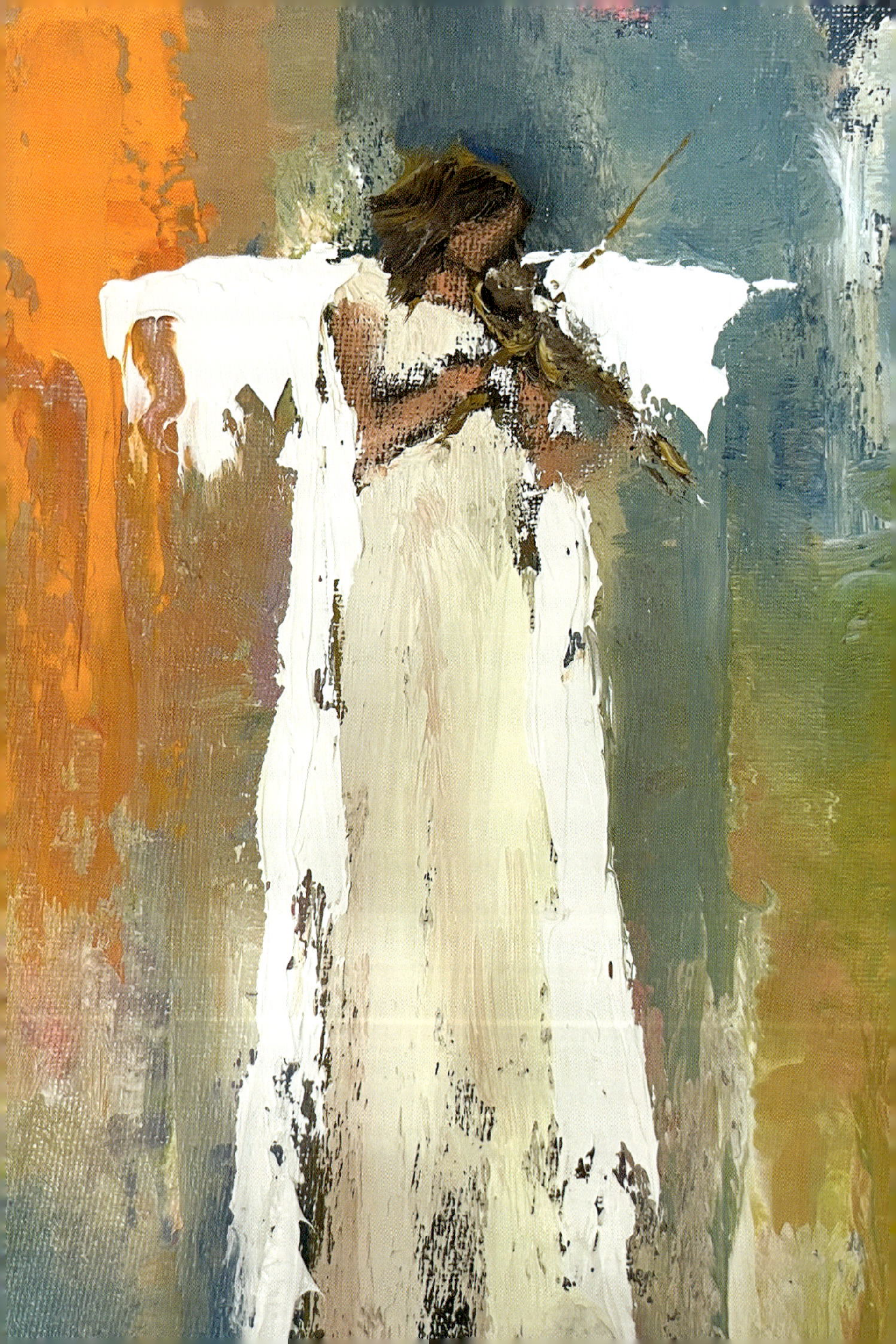

DAY 23

Uniquely Serving God

You will keep in perfect peace
those whose minds are steadfast,
because they trust in you.

Isaiah 26:3

Busy.

I talk about this word a lot in my speaking engagements and reference it often in my devotions. How does the word *busy* resonate with you? Especially today with less than a week to go before Christmas?

It doesn't matter if it is December, May, June, or July—most people say "I am so busy" all year long. I don't want to get caught up in the hustle culture of our world, so I came up with an acronym:

BUSY BUSY
Be Uniquely Serving Yahweh By Using [what is] Specifically Yours.

We are all busy men and women. Whether we are in the corporate world, navigating volunteer roles, coaching Little League, or picking up kids for car pools, we all have roles in the world of busy. But God has given each of us a gift, and that gift is to have open hands and an open heart to serve Him joyfully. Now, I am not saying that we are to say yes to every opportunity that comes our way. I'm saying that as we seek and serve God, He will ultimately guide our steps so that instead of feeling overwhelmed, we will be whelmed over with His peace that passes all understanding.

NOW IS THE PERFECT TIME TO GET BUSY DOING KINGDOM WORK.

What are your gifts during this season that keep you busy but at the same time glorify God? It might be baking for others. It might be serving others who are less fortunate. It might be helping a family who is suffering loss by bringing meals, cleaning, or just being there for them. And if you are not busy, I suggest now is the perfect time to get busy doing kingdom work.

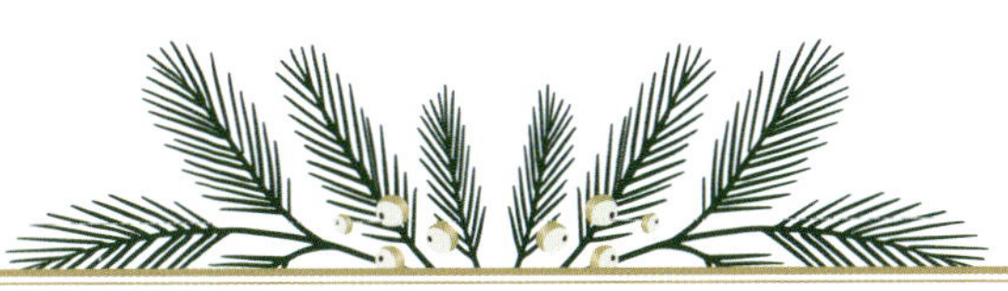

Dear Lord,

Today, I open my hands and surrender this day to You. All the things on my to-do list I give to You. As I walk throughout this day, remind me that You will go before me and guide every step. I want to be uniquely serving You in all that I do. With open hands and an open heart, I thank You that I can reject the hustle culture and be still, knowing that You are God and that You will continue to guide me all day long.

In the name of Jesus,

Amen.

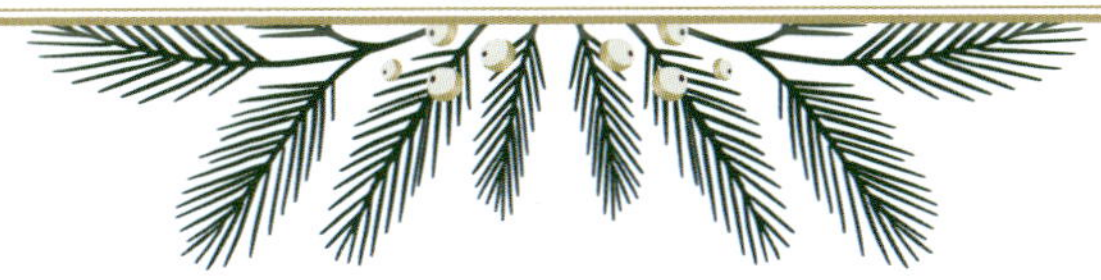

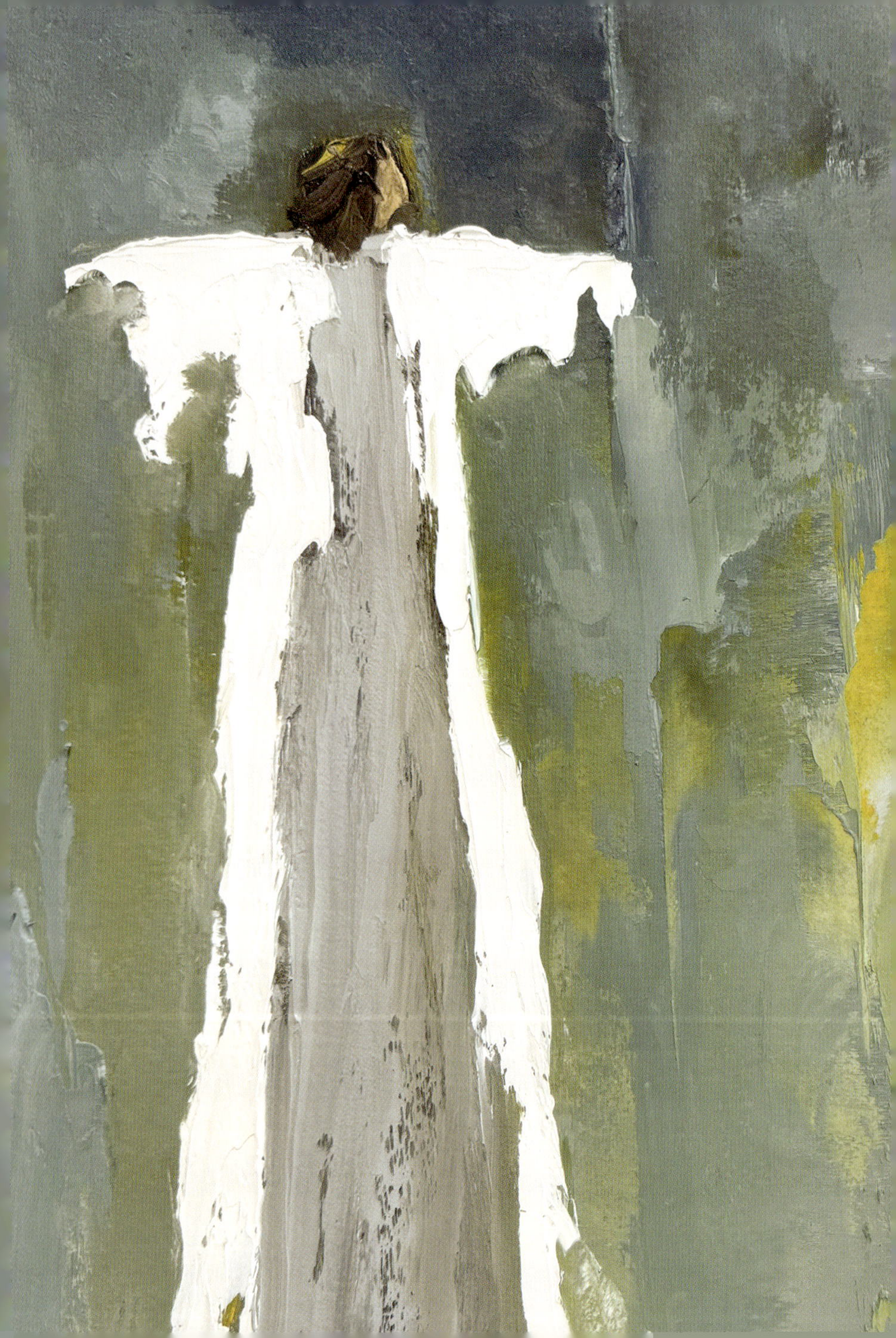

DAY 24

Peace Through the Storm

Lord, you establish peace for us; all that we have accomplished you have done for us.

Isaiah 26:12

It's difficult to watch the news these days and not feel an immense burden of sadness, and maybe even hopelessness, for the state of our country. Current political issues notwithstanding, the seemingly endless list of conflicts, climate disasters, shootings, and increasing racial divides, along with a climate of distrust and insecurity, are impossible to ignore. As believers we shouldn't turn a blind eye to it all, but I find myself wondering how to stand firm in the fire without being engulfed by the flames. How do I battle the inferno when it seems that all I'm holding is a squirt gun? And how do I offer peace to the world now, especially in a season meant for remembrance, celebration, and reflection?

I'm reminded of the Old Testament scripture in Isaiah 43:2, where God assures us that although we will most assuredly walk through fire, He will lead us through it. And when we come out on the other side, we won't even smell like smoke. Wow. Can you picture that? God has equipped us to walk right through the heat of hell without any evidence on the other side.

THE FIRES ARE INEVITABLE, BUT HE WILL GUIDE US THROUGH THEM.

Too often I fall prey to prayers that are too simple. *Lord, please deliver me out of this battlefield.* But just as God delivered the Israelites out of Egypt by leading them through the Red Sea and into the promised land, He will do that for us too.

Maybe God is asking us, when we feel overwhelmed by the issues around us, to know that while the fires are inevitable, He will guide us through them. This Advent I pray that you will find a spirit of peace and a community of loved ones who will lift up your heart and steer you toward peace.

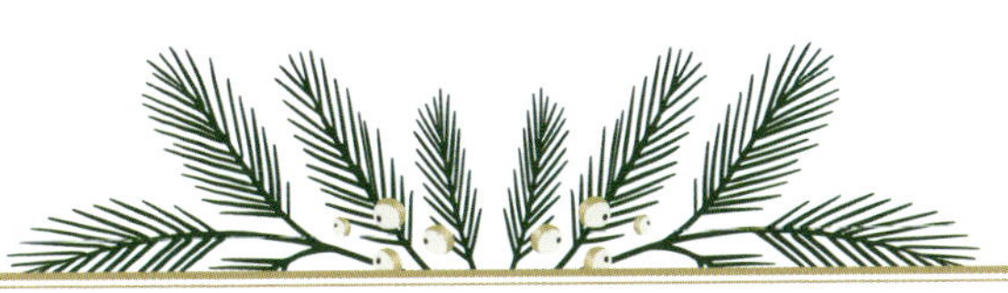

Dear Lord,

As I navigate the storms of my life, I cling to Your promises that You will go before me and Your peace will cover me always and forever. I am ever so grateful for the season I am in right now. No matter what trial I might walk through, I know that when I grab ahold of Your hand, You will guide me. And I thank You that we are in a season in which we celebrate Your ultimate gift, Jesus, the Prince of Peace. I give You glory and thank You for the peace that passes all understanding.

In the name of Jesus,

Amen.

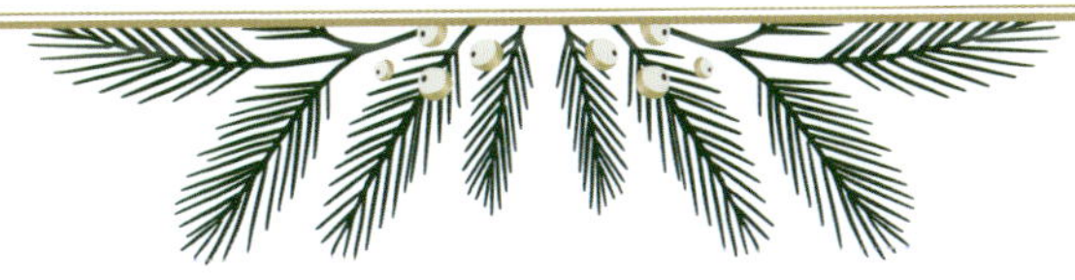

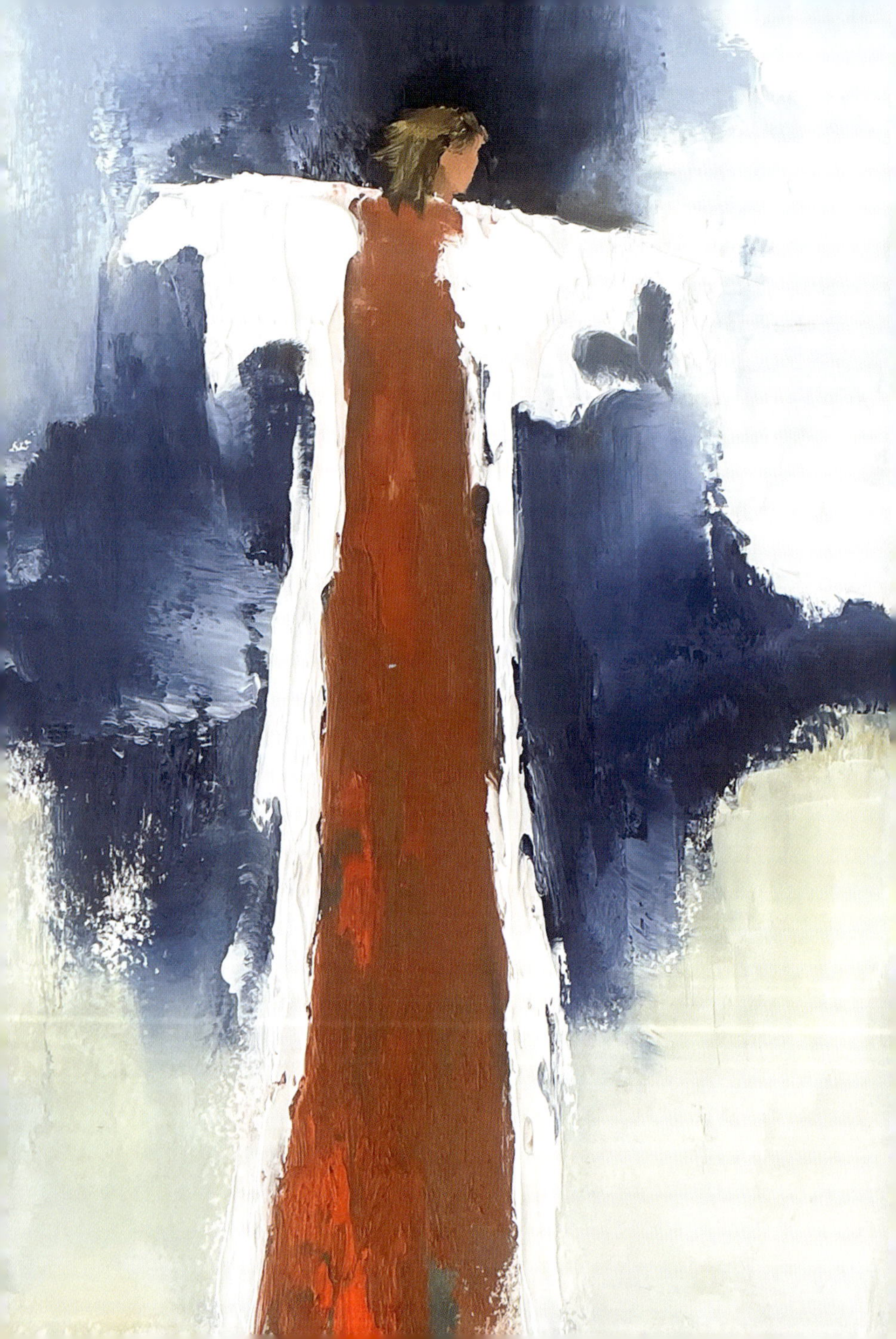

DAY 25

Still, Small Voice

He says, "Be still, and know that I am God;
I will be exalted among the nations,
I will be exalted in the earth."

Psalm 46:10

Did you know that a baby can pick out the sound of its mother's voice in a crowded room of women speaking at the same time?[6] Similarly, sheep know the sound of their shepherd, and they will follow only his commands. Imagine the hum of your shepherd's voice echoing over the sound of hundreds of bleating members of the flock.

It can be difficult to hear God's voice in our busy world and during a chaotic season. It's easy to miss the divinely appointed words the Creator is uttering to you and for you—whether in a still, small whisper, in a thundering shout, or through the words of a close confidant.

I am reminded of a day when I heard the Lord speak so clearly. I was at the beach sitting in the surf and praying when I heard, *What do you want? What do you want in a husband?* Undoubtedly, those questions were being asked by God.

I had been on only ten dates with my then future husband. Several months before, I had asked the Lord to forgive me for taking charge of my life, and I'd surrendered to His will for me. I desperately wanted to be married and have children. I was approaching thirty, and time was ticking. How refreshing to hear Him asking me to tell Him my heart's desires! When I paused to hear from Him and then reply to Him, He heard me and answered with a proposal soon after—and now my house is full of four children.

ONLY WHEN WE PAUSE AND SEEK HIS VOICE WILL WE HEAR IT.

If we strip away the white noise clogging our ears, we can hear the voice of God that has been imprinted on our hearts from our first breath. After all, He created our hearts to beat and our lungs to breathe. His voice isn't unfamiliar; it's in our DNA, but only when we pause and seek His voice will we hear it.

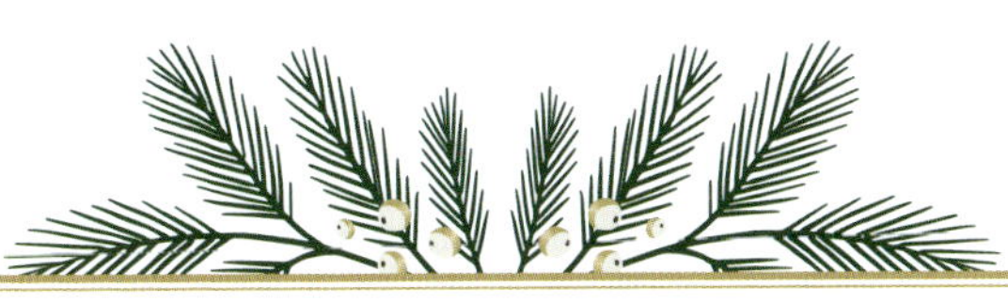

Dear Lord,

Quiet my soul today so I can hear Your still, small voice. The world can get extra loud these days, and throughout this Christmas season, I pray that there would be moments when I hear Your voice and not the voice of the world. Thank You that You would interrupt the busy moments throughout my day to redirect my focus to the true meaning of this Christmas season: Your Son, Jesus, who was born but ultimately died for me.

In the name of Jesus,

Amen.

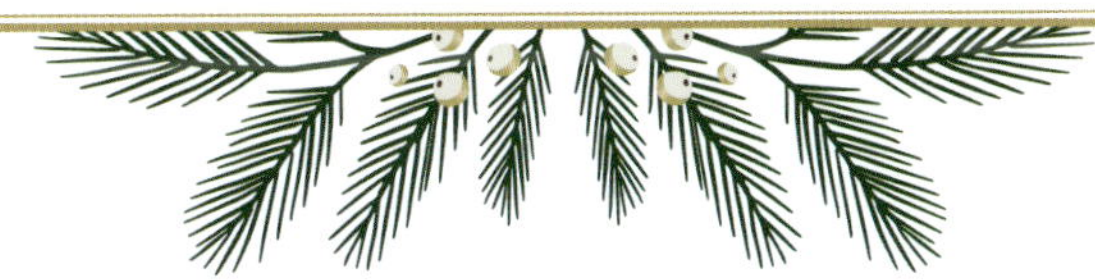

DAY 26

Perfect Peace

"Glory to God in the highest heaven, and on earth peace to those on whom his favor rests."

LUKE 2:14

During the Christmas season, we often hear the familiar proclamation of the angels to the shepherds in Luke 2:14: "Glory to God in the highest heaven, and on earth peace to those on whom his favor rests." This divine declaration not only announced the birth of the Savior but also carries a profound message of peace for all mankind.

God's peace goes beyond the mere absence of conflict or turmoil. It is a deep and abiding sense of tranquility, harmony, and wholeness that can come only from God. This peace is a gift from the Prince of Peace Himself, Jesus Christ, who came to reconcile us to God and bring peace to our restless hearts.

Today, reflect on the message of the angels. Be reminded that true peace is found in a personal relationship with Jesus. In Him we find forgiveness, redemption, and restoration. He is the source of our peace, the One who calms the storms within us and offers us His unshakable peace that passes all understanding.

PAUSE TO RECEIVE THE GIFT OF DIVINE PEACE THAT JESUS OFFERS.

During this Christmas season, amid the hustle and bustle of festivities and the busyness of life, I invite you to pause to receive the gift of divine peace that Jesus offers. Allow His peace to reign in your heart, to guide your steps, and to be a beacon of hope in a world that often feels chaotic and uncertain.

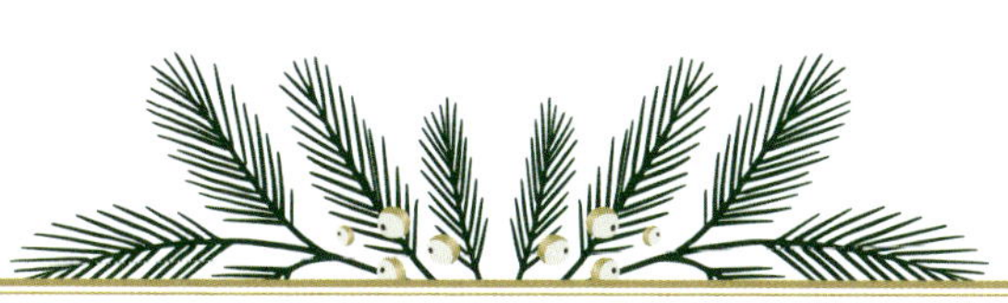

Dear Lord,

As Christmas Day draws closer, and we prepare to celebrate the birth of our Savior, I pray that I would experience the deep and transformative peace that only You can give. May Your peace fill me today with comfort, strength, and joy, knowing that You are with us always, bringing peace on earth and goodwill to all.

In the name of Jesus,

Amen.

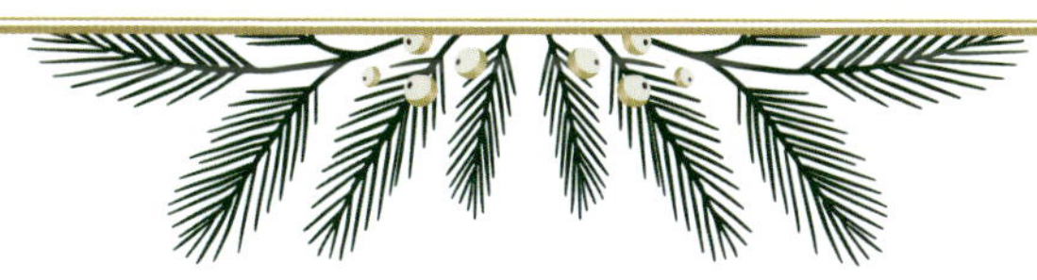

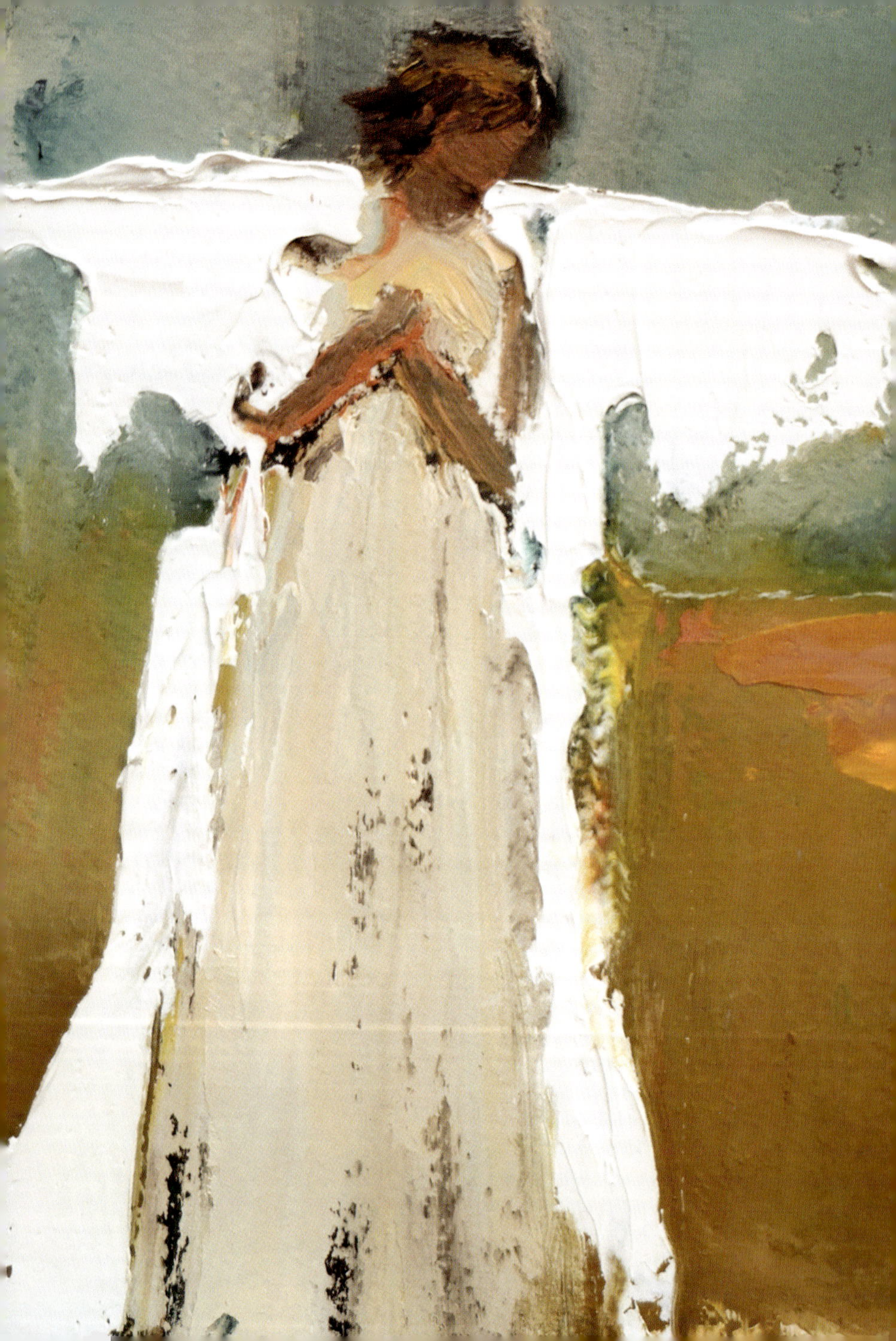

DAY 27

He Is Our Peace

For he himself is our peace.

Ephesians 2:14

In Ephesians 2:14 the apostle Paul beautifully captured the essence of Christmas by proclaiming that Jesus Christ is our peace. Through His birth, His life, His death, and His miraculous resurrection, Jesus brought reconciliation between God and humanity, breaking down the barriers that separated us and making a way for unity and peace.

As we celebrate the birth of Jesus during this Christmas season, we are reminded of the profound impact of His coming to earth as a baby, humble yet divine. Jesus not only bridged the gap between God and us but also tore down the walls of division and hostility that exist among people. In Christ there is no room for animosity, prejudice, or hate. Instead, He brings unity, love, and peace.

The message of Christmas is a message of reconciliation and unity. Just as Jesus reconciled us to God through His sacrificial love, He calls us to be agents of reconciliation and unity in our relationships with others. As followers of Christ, we are called to break down walls of division, to extend forgiveness and grace, and to seek peace with all people.

LET HIS EXAMPLE OF LOVE, HUMILITY, AND SELFLESSNESS INSPIRE US TO BE PEACEMAKERS.

This Christmas, let us reflect on the profound truth that Jesus is our peace. Let His example of love, humility, and selflessness inspire us to be peacemakers in a world that is often filled with conflict and discord. Today, find ways to build bridges, to heal wounds, and to promote understanding and harmony among all people, regardless of differences.

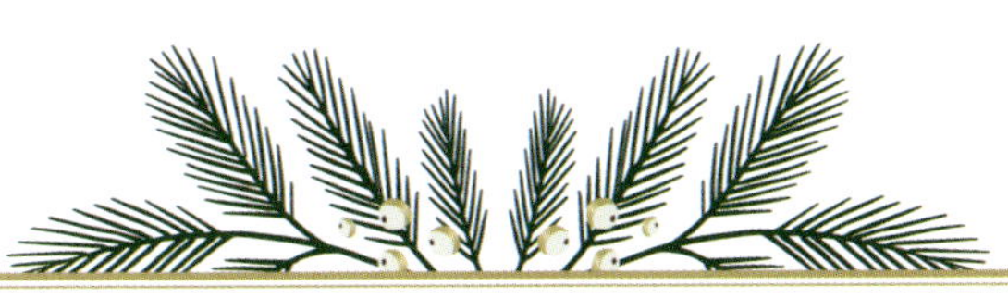

Dear Lord,

Today, I rejoice in the birth of my Savior, Jesus Christ. Let me embrace the call to be an ambassador of peace and unity, reflecting the love of Christ to a world in desperate need of His reconciling power. May the message of peace echo in my heart throughout this day, reminding me of the transformative power of Christ's peace in my life and in the world around me.

In the name of Jesus,

Amen.

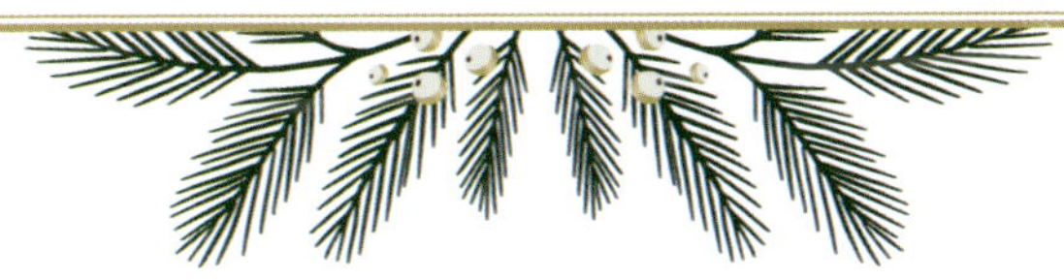

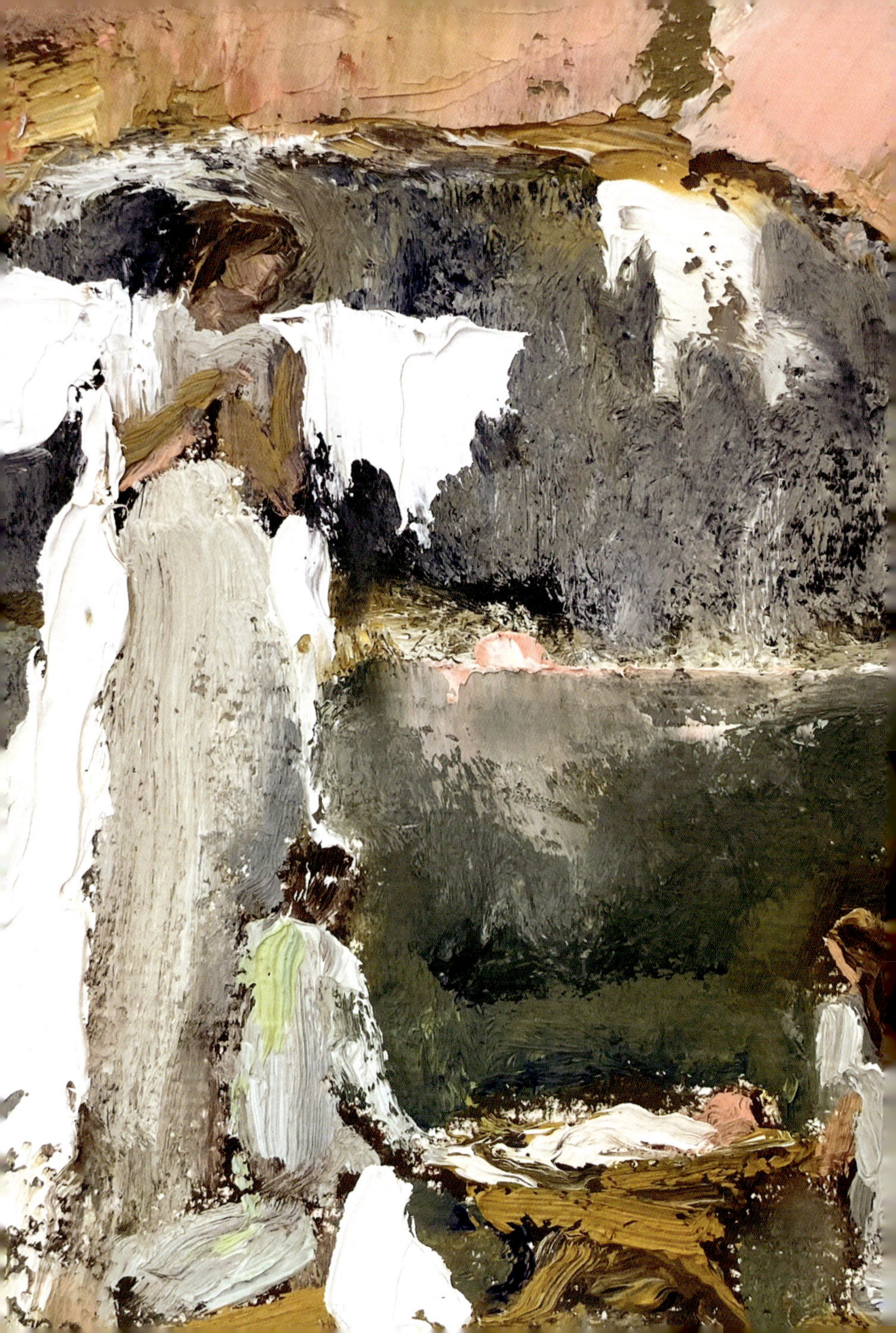

DAY 28

The Ultimate Gift

The beginning of the gospel of Jesus Christ, the Son of God. As it is written in Isaiah the prophet, "Behold, I send my messenger before your face, who will prepare your way, the voice of one crying in the wilderness: 'Prepare the way of the Lord, make his paths straight.'"

MARK 1:1–3 ESV

I had a dear friend many years ago for whom it was very difficult to accept a gift—of any kind. She had suffered some heartaches throughout her life as well as battled depression. I would often show up at her humble home offering prayer and sometimes a meal or gift of some sort. Sheepishly she would push the gifts away, not feeling worthy of receiving them. As I walked away from one of our visits one day, the Lord pressed upon my heart that sometimes gifts get delivered and then are stored on a shelf. Gifts are meant to be opened and unwrapped with great excitement and then enjoyed, not just stored where they'll collect dust.

As you gather today to celebrate the birth of Jesus, reflect on the ultimate gift that you have in Jesus Christ.

The message of Christmas is one of hope and joy. It is a reminder that God kept His promise to send a Savior, His gift to all mankind, who would bring light into the darkness and peace to a troubled world. In the birth of Jesus, we see the ultimate demonstration of God's love for us, as He humbly entered our world to dwell among us.

MAY HIS BIRTH ALWAYS BE A REMINDER OF THE ULTIMATE GIFT AND IMMEASURABLE LOVE HE HAS FOR EACH ONE OF US.

Today, rejoice in the hope that He brings. Don't just open the gift of Jesus and leave Him on the shelf for whenever you need Him.

Continue to marvel at the wonder of God's plan of salvation unfolding before your eyes. May His birth always be a reminder of the ultimate gift and immeasurable love He has for each one of us and the promise of eternal life He offers to all who believe in Him.

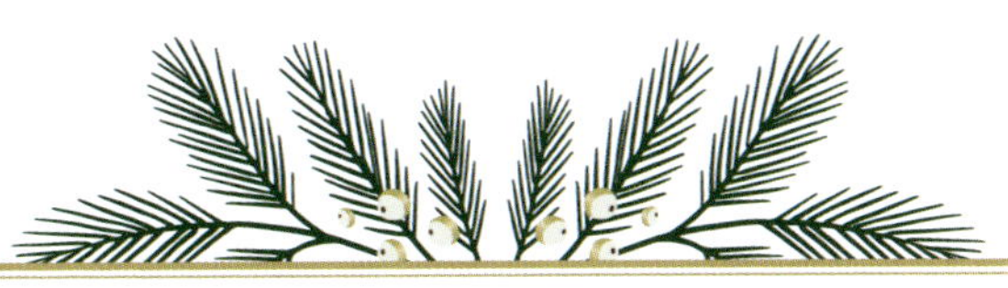

Dear Lord,

As I exchange gifts, share meals, and gather with loved ones on this Christmas Day, let me never forget the greatest gift of all: the gift of Jesus Christ, my Savior and Redeemer. May His presence in my life fill me with peace, joy, and gratitude as I celebrate the miracle of His birth and the hope He brings to the world. Thank You that this Christmas Day is filled with blessings, joy, and the presence of the newborn King. I am rejoicing today and always for the ultimate gift of Jesus!

In the name of Jesus,

Amen.

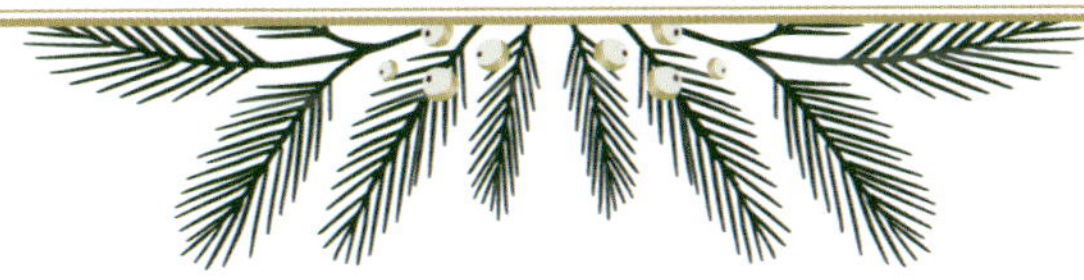

Notes

1. Isaac Watts, "Joy to the World," 1719.
2. Bible Study Tools, "agapao," accessed January 28, 2025, https://www.biblestudytools.com/lexicons/greek/nas/agapao.html.
3. Kathie Lee Gifford, "Bethlehem: Church of the Nativity," FaithGateway.com, accessed February 15, 2025, https://faithgateway.com/blogs/christian-books/bethlehem-church-of-the-nativity.
4. "Keep Your Brain Young with Music," Johns Hopkins Medicine, accessed November 8, 2024, https://www.hopkinsmedicine.org/health/wellness-and-prevention/keep-your-brain-young-with-music.
5. Isaac Watts, "Joy to the World," 1719.
6. Kate Fehlhaber, "How Babies Know Their Mother's Voice—Even in the Womb," *New York Post*, October 23, 2016, https://nypost.com/2016/10/23/how-babies-know-their-mothers-voice-even-in-the-womb/.

Acknowledgments

As I embark on another journey of publishing a book, I am once again filled with gratitude for the incredible support received from so many wonderful people. First and foremost, a shout-out to my family. You are my rock and the heartbeat that keeps me dreaming. I pray that I can always be the cheerleader in your lives as you create, step out in faith, and dream big for your own journeys. As each of you know, family is my everything, and I am so grateful for your love and support along the way. I pray that this Advent devotional will always be a reminder of the true reason for the season and will encourage you to shine the light of Jesus, not just during the Christmas season but throughout the entire year.

To my amazing teams, both at Anne Neilson Home and Anne Neilson Fine Art, your hard work and creativity are invaluable along this journey, allowing me to write, paint, and dream some more. Thank you for your passionate dedication to making both the gallery and the product line something bigger and better every day. I am grateful for each of you!

To my friends and supporters, thank you for your enthusiasm and faith in my writing. I love to hear comments from you about how my writing and vulnerability in sharing my story have deepened your faith journey. Your support means the world to me, and I hope this Advent book brings much joy and inspiration to everyone who reads it.

A heartfelt thank-you goes out to the entire publishing team for believing in this project from the very beginning. Your expertise and commitment have provided the foundation for this book, transforming an idea into a tangible reality. I am grateful for your guidance and the faith you have placed in my work. A big thank-you to Caroline Arey, who composed the beautiful poems for each section. You have a gift with words and bringing those words together in such a beautiful way.

My prayer is that we can all slow down not just during the Advent season but every day throughout the year to draw closer to the King of kings, who was born in a manger, then died on a cross for you and for me. He wants to bring endless hope, unconditional love, abundant joy, and His perfect peace to the world!

Merry Christmas to all!

About the Author

A lifelong artist, Anne Neilson began painting with oils in 2003 and quickly became nationally known for her ethereal Angel Series, which is an inspiring reflection of her faith.

Neilson has published several books, including three coffee table books, *Angels in Our Midst*, *Strokes of Compassion*, and *Angels: The Collector's Edition*. Her latest books, published through Thomas Nelson, include *Anne Neilson's Angels: Devotions and Art to Encourage, Refresh, and Inspire*, *Entertaining Angels: True Stories and Art Inspired by Divine Encounters*, and *The Brushstrokes of Life: Discovering How God Brings Beauty and Purpose to Your Story.*

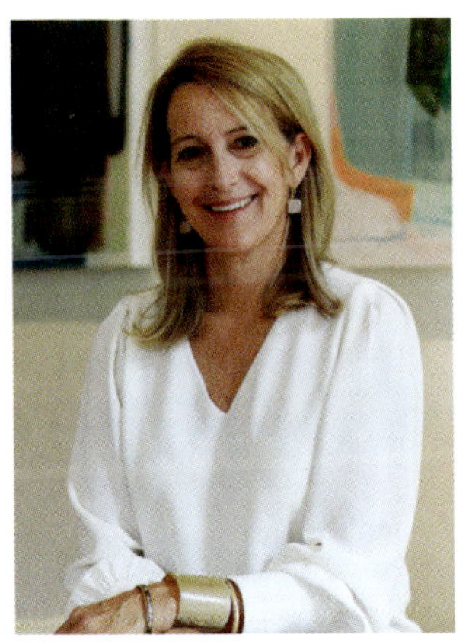

Because of the high demand for her original oils, Anne Neilson Home launched in 2013, which is a collection of luxury home products complementing the Angel Series and providing one-of-a-kind beauty and quality.

In 2014, Neilson opened Anne Neilson Fine Art (ANFA), a gallery located in Charlotte, North Carolina, representing more than sixty artists throughout the country. ANFA showcases masterpieces from the finest artists and shines a light on charitable organizations by donating a portion of art proceeds each month.

With a passion to make a difference in the world, Neilson continues to paint, write, and share her journey through speaking engagements. She is also a wife of twenty-nine years to Clark and a mother of four adult children.

Learn more about Anne Neilson Home,
her luxury home product line, at
www.anneneilsonhome.com | @anneneilsonhome

Learn more about Anne Neilson Fine Art at
www.anneneilsonfineart.com | @anneneilsonfineart

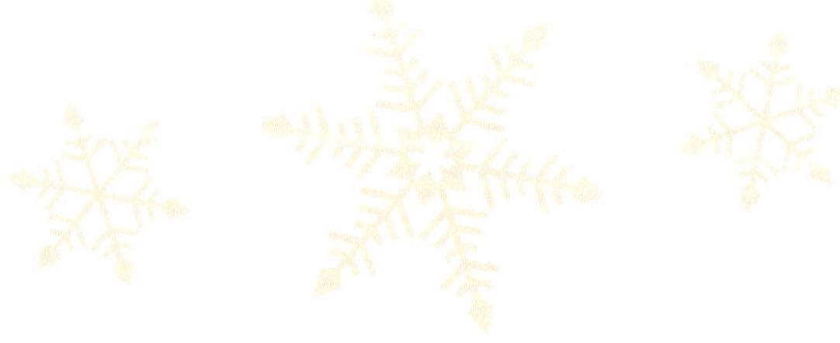